GW00739331

Welcome...

We all know the iPad is great for fun and games, but its potential to boost your career is also huge. Using the 150 apps we've handpicked in this MagBook, you'll learn how your beloved iPad can make you work faster and better, and get you the pay rise you deserve.

If you don't own an iPad, but always thought you should get one, use this MagBook as an excuse to finally buy one. Or, better still, show this to your boss and say you need one to become more productive. With the persuasion tips you'll master in Chapter 5, it might just work.

Daniel Booth, Editor

HOW TO USE THIS MAGBOOK...

We've split this guide into 11 chapters, the first 10 looking at apps to boost your career and financial well-being. In the final chapter we've chosen the best iPad accessories to use in the office, at home and on business trips. After going through the work-related apps, you'll need a break, so at the end of each chapter we've treated you to five brilliant games to play.

After all, it can't always be work, work, work!

What we think the app is best for

The app's icon on your iPad

Its title, price and a link to it in iTunes

WHER

For a regular fix of the best phone and iPad apps, read Web User every fortnight

For Apple tips, news and reviews read MacUser every fortnight

Just search for 'Web User' or 'MacUser' on the Apple Newsstand to find them

Editor Daniel Booth
Contributor Tom Gorham
Art Editor Heather Reeves
Production Editor Iain White
Digital Production Manager Nicky Baker

MANAGEMENT
MagBook Publisher Dharmesh Mistry
Operations Director Robin Ryan
MD of Advertising Julian Lloyd-Evans
Newstrade Director David Barker
Commercial & Retail Director Martin Belson
Managing Director John Garewal
Chief Operating Officer Brett Reynolds
Group Finance Director Ian Leggett
Chief Executive James Tye
Chairman Felix Dennis

MAGBOOK

The MagBook brand is a trademark of Dennis Publishing Ltd.
30 Cleveland St, London W1T 4JD.
Company registered in England.
All material © Dennis Publishing Ltd, licensed by Felden 2012, and may not be reproduced in whole or in part without the consent of the publishers.

iPad Apps for Highly Successful People
ISBN 1-78106-099-1

LICENSING & SYNDICATION
To license this product please contact Carlotta Serantoni on +44 (0) 20 7907 6550 or email carlotta_serantoni@dennis.co.uk

To syndicate content from this product please contact Anj Dosaj Halai on +44(0) 20 7907 6132 or email anj_dosaj-halai@dennis.co.uk

LIABILITY
While every care was taken during the production of this MagBook, the publishers cannot be held responsible for the accuracy of the information or any consequence arising from it. Dennis Publishing takes no responsibility for the companies advertising in this MagBook.

The paper used within this MagBook is produced from sustainable fibre, manufactured by mills with a valid chain of custody.

Printed at BGP

CONTENTS

Create better presentation p70

iPad accessories to make work easier p114

Get Promoted p18

Mastering iWork

Your iPad has its own suite of apps for handling word processing, page layout, spreadsheets and presenting on the move. Known individually as Pages, Numbers and Keynote, and collectively as iWork, these brilliant apps mean you'll always be able to stay on top of work on the go

I f Microsoft Office is the software suite of choice in corporate desktop environments, Apple's inexpensive suite of iWork apps could lay claim to a similar position in the mobile workplace.

After all, this suite of three brilliant apps, each sold separately for £6.99, offers just about everything you need to keep on top of things on the go.

iWork's most popular app is Pages, a powerful template-based word processor and page-layout tool. Numbers, an advanced spreadsheet app, takes care of the financial side of things, while the presentation package Keynote handles all the marketing. But while the features of each of these apps may be powerful, they're also extremely easy for newcomers to get to grips with.

Thankfully, the way you work with documents is the same in all three apps. In each, you create and manage your own documents through each app's document library. It's a simple, but clever organisational tool that holds all the documents you've created in one place.

Creating a new document is as easy as tapping the big '+' button, at the top, while to open a document you've already created, you just tap the thumbnail preview.

Each app makes it easy to create good-looking documents by offering a

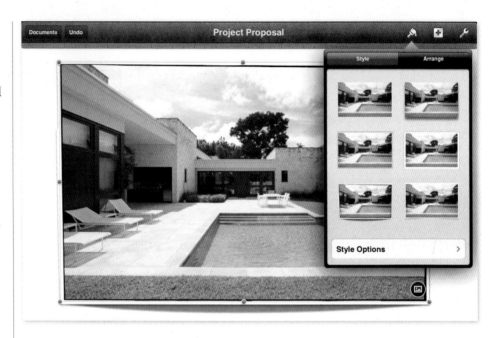

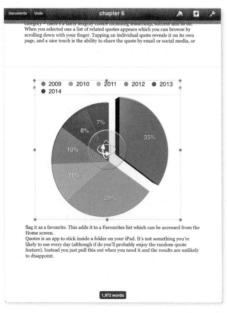

You can open documents saved in native Word, Excel or PowerPoint format in iWork. And it works the other way around too

selection of pre-built templates onto which you can drop your own material. Many of these templates are business-orientated; for example there are Numbers templates for business plans, Pages ones for business letters and CVs and more than 40 Keynote template themes for presentations.

But even if you're building a document from scratch, the same authoring approach applies in all three apps. If you tap inside a text area, the iPad's software keyboard automatically pops up, ready to go. But as the keyboard is software based, its contents can change depending on the context within which it's being used. In Numbers, for example, the keyboard contains special keys which

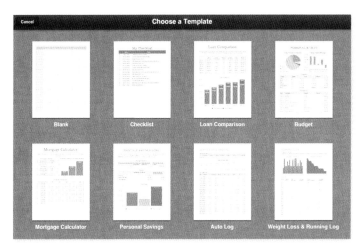

Many of these templates are business-orientated. For example, there are Numbers templates for business plans, Pages ones for business letters and CVs and more than 40 Keynote template themes for presentations

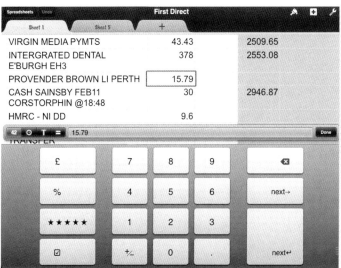

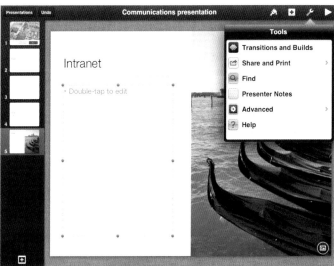

make it easier when entering figures or complex formulas.

Another quick tap on the document bar at the top of the window and you can add shapes, charts and tables to the page, or even import images from your iPad's camera right onto your page. You drag the image to move it on the page or resize it by dragging its corners with your finger.

iWork is well tailored to hands-on mobile use in other ways too. In all three apps, changes are saved as you go, so you don't need to fiddle about looking for a 'Save' button.

Another great feature is if you've set up iCloud syncing through Apple's online cloud service, you can share documents between apps on iPad and iPhone (the same app will work on both devices).

If you have iWork on a Mac, you can also sync to a desktop computer. iCloud isn't, of course, the only way you can do this: you can also sync documents through iTunes or any WebDAV-compatible server.

But what really makes iWork a worthwhile buy is its compatibility. You don't need to worry if you're working with colleagues who are using Microsoft Office, because you can open documents saved in native Word, Excel or PowerPoint format in iWork. And it works the other way around too: the iWork documents you create on your iPad can also easily be shared in Office format.

THE 10 BEST THINGS...
YOU CAN DO IN iWORK

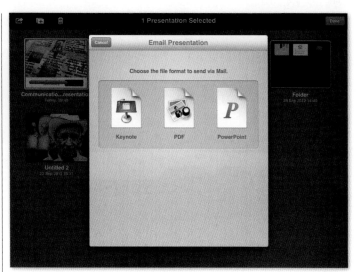

1 Create interactive documents

Don't think of Keynote just as any presentation app; it's far more versatile than that. You can also use it to make interactive documents because any element in a Keynote slide can be made into a hyperlink. When the object is tapped, this hyperlink can transfer the user to another slide in the same presentation or a website, or even open an email.

2 Create a publication on the go

Want to send a business update to contacts on the move? Capture images (or even video) using your iPad's camera, import it into a Pages template from the camera roll, and then when you're finished editing, export it from the Document Library as a PDF. Finally, to share it, open Mail, enter the addresses of your business contacts and hit send. Easy!

3 Sharing with colleagues

iCloud is a great way to keep documents in sync, but to share yours with a team, you can store them on your office server if it's WebDAV-enabled. You can then open these files when you're on the move with your iPad, knowing that all your colleagues will have access to the same up-to-date files back in the office.

4 Form-filling

In Numbers you can edit in a special Forms view of your spreadsheets data. This offers chunky navigation buttons, checkboxes and sliders, which makes it really easy to enter small amounts of data into a larger spreadsheet. Underneath, it's still a fully fledged spreadsheet, so all the data entered can be analysed later.

5 Wireless printing

Thanks to AirPrint technology, you can print from the Share menu in any iWork app. Many recent HP printers are AirPrint-compatible, but if your printer isn't, then don't worry as some handy software (FingerPrint 2 on a PC, www.collobos.com, Printopia 2 on a Mac, www.ecamm.com/mac/printopia), lets your iPad share your PC's printer.

6 Present anywhere

Using iWork on an iPad means you don't need to carry around a laptop and a copy of PowerPoint if you want to give a presentation on the move. Armed with a suitable adapter to connect to a projector (likely to be either VGA or HDMI), your iPad can turn into a big-screen presentation machine in the blink of an eye.

7 Open Office files

Don't worry if you receive an email with Microsoft Word or Excel attachments. Just tap their thumbnail previews to open them in the appropriate iWork app. iWork does a good job of converting files, and when it comes to sending them back to Office-using colleagues, simply select the Share option from the Document Library and choose the relevant Office export option.

8 Use Kiosk mode

Keynote's Kiosk mode is a great way to show off a multimedia presentation at an exhibit or other event. In the Tools menu, go to Advanced, Presentation Type. Choose to loop the presentation and select the 'Self-Playing' option.

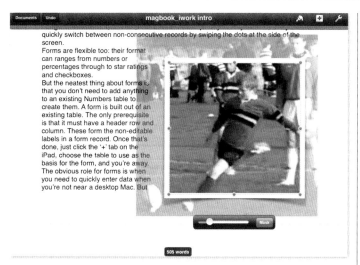

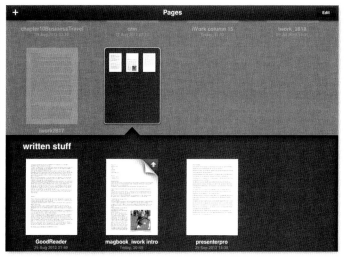

9 Mask images

You can give images more impact by masking them to crop unwanted elements. It's simple to do and it helps make your layouts more eye-catching. To define a mask, simply double-tap an image in your document and use the slider that appears to resize the image within the mask.

10 Smart organisation

The Document Library can appear limited at first glance, but you can easily knock it into shape by creating folders within it. Simply tap and hold the thumbnail preview of one document and then drag it over another to create a new folder containing both documents.

Find a lost iPad

Accidentally left your iPad in the back of a taxi after an important business meeting? You're stuffed, right? Not necessarily. Increase your chances of being reunited with the help of iCloud's Find My iPad service, which locates it on a map and either locks or wipes it remotely

Apple recognises that businesspeople take their iPads everywhere they go, so there's always a chance they could lose it. This might be completely innocent, as we could leave it on the train or in a meeting room, or it could be more malicious. Thieves are always on the lookout for easy-to-steal expensive hi-tech equipment – from cameras to mobile phones – and in any big city, an unguarded iPad makes a prime target.

However you happen to be parted from your iPad, you want the best chance of finding it again; or, if it's been taken dishonestly, at least removing your sensitive data to keep it safe from prying eyes. That's where the brilliantly useful Find My iPad (bit.ly/findmyipadinfo) comes in.

What is Find My iPad?

Find My iPad is a smart service that uses iCloud to locate your iPad anywhere in the world using its GPS chip or an active Wi-Fi connection.

It relies on you having at least one iCloud email account active on the device, which is set to receive push email. If you don't have this set up, tap Settings, Mail, Contacts, Calendars, Add Account… and select iCloud from the list of options. Find My iPad is turned off by default. This

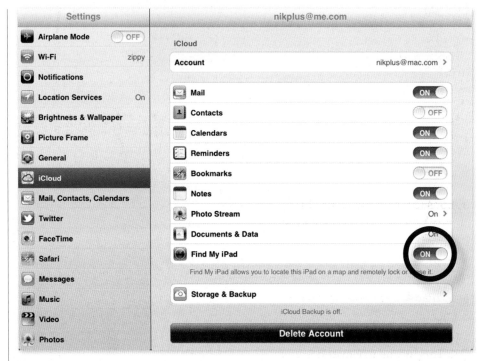

makes sense because it relies on passing your current location through the iCloud servers, which some users may consider to be a security risk. It's simple to turn on, though. Tap Settings, iCloud and tap the ON/OFF slider beside Find My iPad (above).

Log in to your iCloud account at icloud.com using a regular browser and click the icon in the top-left corner to open the iCloud apps menu. Select Find My iPhone. The app works for iPhones as well as iPads and MacBooks. It should really be called the more accurate 'Find My iDevice'.

Right away iCloud starts searching for each of the devices that you've registered to your account and plotting them on a map. You can switch between them by clicking each one in the My Devices panel, and switch between zoomable map, satellite and hybrid views to help you zoom in to the closest location.

Select the device that you need to locate – in our case an iPad – and it will be highlighted on the map with a small pop-up bubble protruding from a pushpin. Clicking the blue 'i' at the end of the bubble gives you three

options for remotely controlling your device: sending a message, remotely locking it or wiping it completely.

Your first step should be to send a message, which will be displayed on your iPad's screen the next time it connects to the internet along with a loud beeping, until the viewer taps OK. This means whoever has your iPad can't claim that they didn't know it had been lost or stolen.

Include in this message whatever details would help facilitate the return of your iPad, but be careful not to give away too many personal details or put yourself at risk by organising a meeting in unsafe circumstances. By default, iCloud will have set the option to play a sound at the same time as displaying the message.

If this doesn't yield a successful result then you should move on to the next steps: either locking or wiping it.

When locked, the iPad can only be unlocked using your existing security

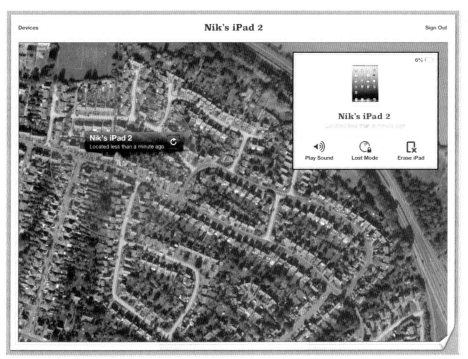

code. If you have set your iPad to wipe after 10 unsuccessful entries then you already have another level of security built in. Your last line of defence is the remote wipe via

icloud.com. You should only do this if you're sure that you're not going to get your iPad back because it's impossible to locate it again using Find My iPad once it's been wiped.

CHAPTER 1
GET A PAY RISE

BEST APP FOR...
NEGOTIATING YOUR SALARY

Jobjuice-Salary Negotiation • £10.49 • bit.ly/jobjuiceipadapp

Jobjuice is a great little app for boosting your chances of getting a pay rise. The app is arranged into five sections, most of which provide advice on how to squeeze more money when negotiating for a job offer, or how to get a pay rise while remaining in the same one. The sections are organised into a simple list view, which you tap to reveal individual topic cards.

Many tips are extremely useful, such as how to anticipate and overcome the two most common objections to a salary increase: the

company can't afford it, and your performance doesn't merit it. Another tip explains why you should never say yes to the first pay offer.

There's a lot of material to work with but, helpfully, related topics are hyperlinked, so you don't get lost. The menu bar at the bottom of the screen links to a selection of cards devoted to a handful of tactics you can use to encourage the other side to agree to your demands. And as general negotiating advice, there are seven useful tactics to use as introductory gambits when you start.

The app offers a way to hone your negotiating skills by revealing a card's title, which you then tap to reveal its content. So, with a little study, you'll quickly become an expert on using techniques like the Vise gambit ("I'm sorry, you'll have to do better than that") or the 'silent close' technique.

Jobjuice isn't a cheap option and may initially seem daunting, but the material within it is excellent and will be useful far beyond negotiating with your manager. And you can always put the price of the app down as an investment against future earnings.

BEST APP FOR...
DISCOVERING YOUR WORTH

Salary Checker • Free • bit.ly/salarychecker

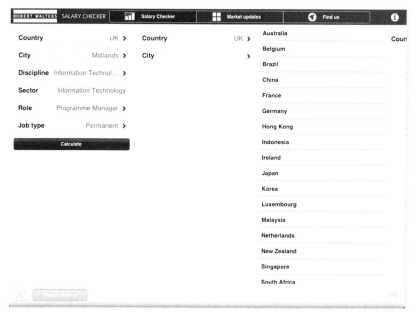

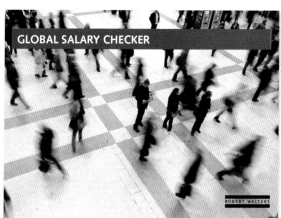

The process of asking for a raise can be a game of cat and mouse with your boss, but you can put yourself in the driving seat by finding out what your peers in the same industry earn elsewhere.

Finding out your colleagues' salaries can be a taboo area, but the Salary Checker app gives an unbiased and up-to-date picture of what you might expect for a given position in a range of countries. The results can be such an eye-opener that this app may end up being more than a handy pay-rise tool; it might even make you consider starting a new career abroad.

Salary Checker organises the results of a 2012 global salary survey into an app. Once you've tapped successive buttons to choose your location (country and area), discipline, sector, role and job type, Salary Checker shows the range of salaries for that

position. It also compares the current average salary over the last three years: a rising chart is a good indication that your selected role is in demand. With a quick tap you can share the results via Facebook, Twitter and LinkedIn, although it may be wise to keep your findings to yourself before your pay-review meeting.

Salary Checker has an extensive database but it isn't perfect. In the UK, for example, comparative salaries are only available for some parts of the country, and not all jobs are covered. But there's enough breadth in the type of area included to give you a fair idea of what an average salary might be where you work.

> The results can be such an eye-opener that this app might make you consider taking up a more lucrative career abroad

BEST APP FOR...
WINNING NEW CLIENTS

Shhmooze • Free • bit.ly/shhmoozeipadapp

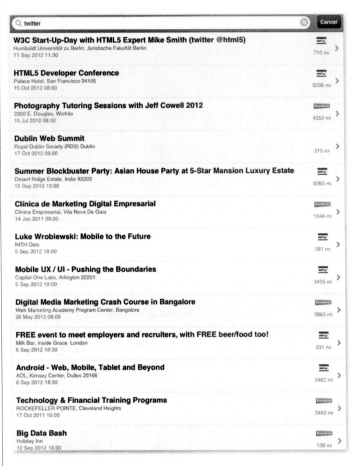

Mixing with the movers and shakers in your area of business is a great way to step up the career ladder or find new opportunities for personal growth. While you can make contacts on social media, networking face-to-face provides the best way to introduce yourself to new customers. Shhmooze bridges both types of networking by finding local events that people you know are attending.

It does this cleverly, first by using Location Awareness in your iPad to work out where you are. It then integrates with popular event-organising services to present a huge list of what's happening locally. As soon as you confirm your attendance at an event by tapping the event's name in a list and checking in, you can see who else is going.

Shhmooze links with your Foursquare, LinkedIn and Twitter accounts if your contacts are attending an event. You can send them a secure message to set up a meeting, and an in-app inbox lets you read messages from others. Even more impressively from a career-enhancing perspective, you can check out the profile of attendees you don't know so you can be well prepared to impress them with more than just a handshake.

The best thing about Shhmooze is how unobtrusive it is. There's no requirement to sign up for events: a simple check in will give you a list of attendees as well as a map of the event and more details. And because it's taking profile information from other social-media applications, other attendees don't need to be running Shhmooze. Setting it up is easy. In fact, once this app has permission to access your social-media accounts, Shhmooze will build a profile for you based on your other social-media profiles.

BEST APP FOR...
NAILING JOB INTERVIEWS

Confident Job Interview · £2.99 · bit.ly/confidentipadapp

> Want to come across better? This app delivers self-confidence in bucketloads, thanks to the power of hypnotherapy

Even if you're well-prepared for all the questions an interviewer might throw at you during a job interview, there's still one hurdle to overcome – self-confidence. Many job seekers just don't have enough, but that's where this app comes in.

You may be capable of doing the job you're being interviewed for, but you may fail to get it because you forget your well-rehearsed answers when faced with a tough interview.

It's no surprise then, that self-confidence is one of the most important attributes that any would-be interviewee can have. And

this app delivers self-confidence in bucketloads, thanks to the power of hypnotherapy. To start, watch the videos explaining the role and usefulness of hypnotherapy, which is a useful primer for anyone worried about how it works. Then listen to the 10 hypnosis tracks, which you can either play in order, which the app recommends, or individually. Just tap the button and listen. Each one is accompanied by a video background of your choice, from night sky to waterfall, which helps you relax.

Two 20-minute 'Confident Job Interview' sessions lie at the core of

this app. One is designed to be listened to during the day, the other last thing at night. After listening to them and absorbing the information, you'll actually be looking forward to the interview, not dreading it.

In fact, sub-par performance under pressure will soon become a thing of the past. There are also generous complementary sessions, including a couple to help you deal with anxiety, which will be useful elsewhere in the workplace, and a further session to help you totally relax in 10 minutes – just the sort of thing to listen to before you leave for your big interview.

BEST APP FOR...
BLITZING YOUR WORKLOAD

OmniFocus for iPad • £13.99 • bit.ly/omnifocusforipad

As you rise through company ranks you'll inevitably be burdened with more tasks that need to be completed to ever-more demanding deadlines. How you handle the pressure will go some way to determining whether you reach the very top. OmniFocus is a great way to organise your important work projects so they're delivered on time, while you keep your sanity.

You can add a task to OmniFocus through its quick-entry window faster than you could jot it down on a piece of paper. At the same time you can add useful metadata, such as assigning a due date to the task, attaching an image or recording a brief audio note using the iPad's microphone. It's all much quicker and efficient than scrawling in a notebook. Once that's done, the task appears in your inbox, on the right-hand side of the screen in landscape mode, until you tap it to mark it as done.

OmniFocus is more than a simple task-gatherer, though. You can also assign groups of related tasks to various projects and tap the Projects button on the left-hand side to see all your tasks together.

Both tasks and projects can have a context assigned to them. Contexts act like tags to link similar tasks in different projects. That's really useful if you need to work on a task or a project at a particular time. Create a context called 'Do first thing Monday' and everything you've tagged with that context is shown.

But contexts are more powerful than tags because you can add location information to them. As long as you have Location Services enabled on an iPad 2 or later with 3G, OmniFocus can remind you of a task when you enter or leave a particular location. This means, for example, that you can be reminded to hand in that all-important report on Friday before you leave work. OmniFocus requires you to adopt a disciplined way of working, but the time it saves should quickly recoup the investment. And crucially, when your pay-rise meeting arrives, you'll be able to talk about loads of completed projects.

PUT YOUR FEET UP WITH THE...
5 BEST RACING GAMES

1 Real Racing 2 HD · £4.99 · bit.ly/racingipad

Drive 30 cars in this electrifying 3D racer, including five BMWs, five Chevrolets, two McLarens and two Jaguars. You'll need to take a day off work for the massive 10-hour Career mode, but make sure you're not relying on battery power.

2 Lane Splitter

69p · bit.ly/lanesplitterapp
How fast are your reflexes? You'll soon find out playing Lane Splitter, as you have to guide your motorcycle through traffic, dodging cars, walls and cops. Touch the screen to perform wheelies.

3 DrawRace 2

£1.99 · bit.ly/drawracegame
Now, this is ingenious. Trace your finger around one of the 36 tracks as quickly as you can, then your car will follow the route. Much trickier than it sounds as well as highly addictive.

4 Asphalt 6: Adrenaline

£2.99 · bit.ly/asphaltgame
These cars will have you drooling. Choose from Ferraris, Lamborghinis, Aston Martins, Ducatis and Bentleys among others. Locations include Monte Carlo, New York and Cape Town.

5 Final Freeway 2R

69p · bit.ly/freewaygame
If you grew up on the chunky graphics of OutRun, you'll love Final Freeway. Just pick one of the three characters, choose a difficulty level, and you're off. Fast and frenetic retro thrills in spades.

CHAPTER 2
GET PROMOTED

BEST APP FOR...
MAKING YOURSELF INDISPENSABLE

Yammer • Free • bit.ly/yammeripadapp

In today's economic climate, just holding on to your job is challenging enough, let along winning a promotion. But one way you can ensure you rise through the ranks is to get involved with several projects throughout the company, making yourself indispensable. That's quite an aspiration, but how does it work in real life? The social-media service Yammer will help.

Rising in popularity in offices, Yammer is like a business version of Facebook and Twitter. Owned by Microsoft, it offers a private and secure network, so it's ideal for sharing ideas throughout your company.

Any colleague can post their own message or comment to Yammer's company-wide feed, which is a great opportunity to get yourself noticed. Who knows? You might end up in a chat with your managing director.

Like Twitter, you can also follow individuals' posts, so you can keep on top of what your boss is up to. But the best aspect, from a career-development point of view, is the ability to join and create restricted-access groups so you can share information solely within a team, or with like-minded people elsewhere in the company. If you have a great idea, you can bounce it around here and,

after considering suggestions from other well-read colleagues, present a tested proposal to management.

Yammer's app is far easier to use than its website (www.yammer.com). You can quickly flip between your company feed, groups, notifications and private messages from a menu. As you tap a post the conversation that follows appears next to it, and this can be navigated by scrolling with your finger and tapping a button to reply or simply 'like' a comment. And as Yammer isn't hosted on your company's servers, you can still connect to it on the train home. Now *that's* networking on the go.

BEST APP FOR...
LEARNING NEW WORK SKILLS

iTunes U • Free • bit.ly/itunesuipadapp

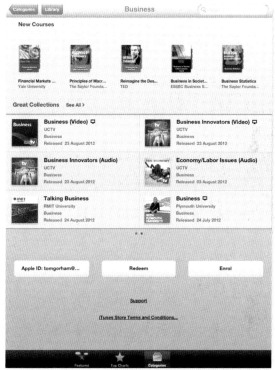

I t's hard to believe that iTunes U was once an unassuming collection of podcasts hidden away on the iTunes Store. Now it's the world's biggest resource of free educational content with an inspiring collection of video, audio and books, all supported by leading universities.

However, don't assume iTunes U is just for aspiring students as among its wide range of topics sits a Business section, which contains a wealth of material to boost your career. Among the gems you'll find videos on effective leadership, and an Oxford

University course on building a business. And they're all free.

To get to the goodies, browse popular courses or search for a topic by using the iTunes-like menu bar at the bottom of the screen. You can then subscribe in a tap, although you can just as easily download videos that interest you. The benefit of subscribing means that course updates will download automatically.

When you subscribe, the course immediately appears in the app's bookshelf. Open this and a virtual binder appears, showing details about

the course's syllabus and instructions. From a bottom menu bar, you'll find links to the course's resources, such as lectures, videos and documents. As you read books, or play audio or video content, you can add your own notes. By keeping all your content together, it really does feel like you have a huge, almost limitless learning resource at your fingertips.

Given the universally excellent quality of the material available, iTunes U is the closest thing that a learning resource can come to a no-brainer download.

BEST APP FOR...
LEARNING SUCCESSFUL HABITS

Habits Pro • 69p • bit.ly/habitsipadapp

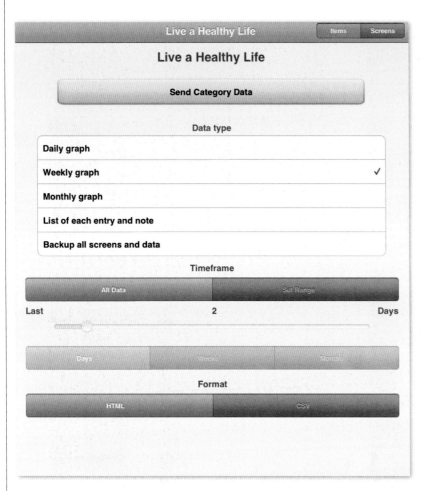

> Posting your progress to Twitter – and introducing peer pressure – provides a powerful incentive to succeed

Because a habit is something we do almost automatically, if we learn how to make it more effective we can become more productive without really trying.

It's turning effective behaviour into a habit that's the tough part. There's something of a scarcity of good iPad apps for this purpose, but while its interface is too complicated, Habits Pro certainly has the best features.

First, you create separate entries for each habit you want to form, such as performing a particular task at work, completing an hour's study each evening or remembering to compliment your boss every morning. These items appear together in a list next to a calendar, and each day you check off whether or not you performed that particular activity.

Over time, the calendar builds up a clear picture of how well you're sticking to your habits. By switching to a graph mode at the bottom of the screen, you can see, in daily, weekly or monthly views, how much of your goal for each habit you managed to achieve over that period in either percentage terms or hard numbers.

Working on refining (or breaking) habits takes self-discipline and the ability to focus on the task in hand. But being able to post your progress to Twitter, thereby opening yourself up to peer pressure, provides another powerful incentive to succeed.

Habits Pro can cope with plenty of different habits at once, so you can also use it to manage your tasks. If you're tracking lots of habits, you can put them into separate categories to be tracked separately. You can easily switch between categories from the menu at the bottom of the screen.

BEST APP FOR...
SETTING AND HITTING NEW GOALS

SimpleGoals • Free • bit.ly/simplegoalsipadapp

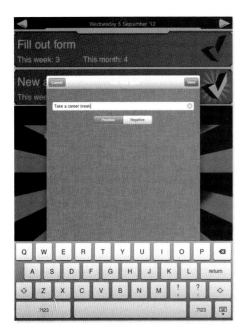

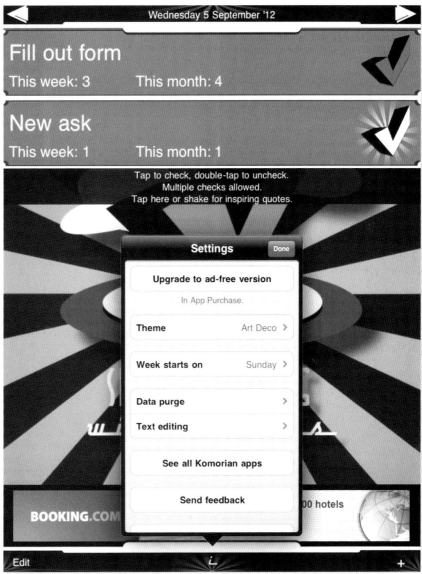

Wonderfully easy to use, SimpleGoals is a single-task app to track how you achieve your goals. To set a goal, you tap the '+' button at the bottom of the screen, enter the name of the goal and whether it's positive or negative. In other words, whether you want to achieve the goal, or avoid doing it.

The goal then appears in a list on your screen under the current date. When you achieve it, you simply tap its name in the list to turn the adjacent tick box green. Handily, you can tap the goal name multiple times to record the fact that you've achieved your target more than once. That makes for an really elegant way to track a cumulative daily goal – such as a sales target, for example.

The goal remains on the list until you remove it through the app's edit button. So when you open the app the next day, the same goal appears, once more freshly unchecked. The previous days' achievements haven't been lost, though. Underneath each task the app displays how many times you've achieved that particular goal during the current week and month, so long-term targets are catered for too. It couldn't be simpler or easier to use.

SimpleGoals has one more impressive feature. Tapping below the list of goals reveals an invariably witty and insightful quote from inspirational figures, such as Leonardo da Vinci and Alexander Graham Bell, that will either motivate you to achieve your daily goals, or make you feel better if you don't.

BEST APP FOR...
STUDYING FOR AN MBA

Pocket MBA: Learning Studio • £13.99 • bit.ly/pocketmbaipadapp

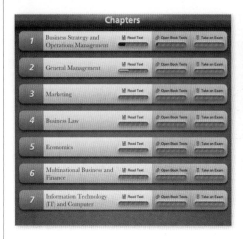

Such is the MBA's cachet that possessing the qualification is often seen a passport to a promotion – it also makes you attractive to external head-hunters.

But it's a tough exam, and you'll need help to pass it. Pocket MBA is the best app to help you do that. Its main screen is divided into seven chapters, beginning with business strategy and operations management and ending with information technology. For each you can select to read the text, or take one of two tests.

The text comprises the contents of a high-quality textbook, divided into multiple topic chapters which you can switch between from a menu on the left (it can be hidden from view so you can concentrate on the content). The app tracks how much of the topic you've completed – you can bookmark sections – while a glossary defines the business terms used.

There are two types of test, both of which include multiple-choice questions. The open-book exam not only lets you see the answers, but also

explains the wrong ones. It's a great way of testing your knowledge in the early stages of study. The exam test is far stricter and only displays the results of the test when you've answered all the questions, simulating the pressure you'd feel in a real exam.

Back on the main screen, bars show how far you've progressed in your studies, and handily illustrate any poorly covered areas that are in need of some extra revision.

By the time your real exam comes along, you should be well prepared.

BEST APP FOR...
UNDERSTANDING THE ECONOMY

The Economist for iPad • Free • bit.ly/theeconomistipadapp

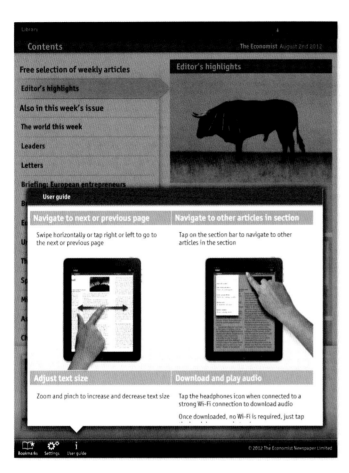

It helps to be an all-rounder if you want a promotion. Mastering the practical mechanics of your current job just shows that you can do it very well. But those who rise to the top have a better all-round grasp of wider economic issues. In short, they know how all the pieces fit together.

But getting that knowledge isn't down to blind luck. More often than not, it's thanks to patient study or appropriate background reading – which is where this app really comes into its own. The essential analysis in *The Economist* is an excellent way to see the bigger picture and get insights into external businesses and economic forces that might affect your business's future.

While you can download a small selection from each issue for free, you'll only get the full content through a digital or print subscription, or by buying individual copies of the magazine (either digital or print) through a £4.99 in-app purchase.

The digital version of the magazine offers several advantages over its paper equivalent. For a start, all your issues of *The Economist* can be kept together; you swipe along the carousel display to choose which issue to open.

And each issue is superbly easy to navigate: tap the menu on the left-hand side of the screen to go to the article, and swipe through pages to move through each story. Cleverly, only text is resized as you zoom, leaving the layout otherwise unaffected, so it's easier to read.

Better still, though, you can download an audio version of the entire magazine over Wi-Fi, and by tapping a button above the current article you can have it read back to you. That turns out to be a fantastic way to get the benefits of the magazine while on your commute.

BEST APP FOR...
IMPRESSING PEOPLE IN MEETINGS

Mgmt Cards • Free • bit.ly/mgmtipadapp

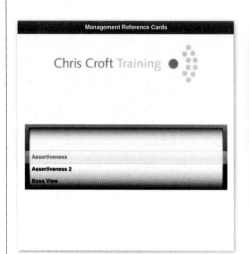

These cards have been created by Chris Croft. CC is a management trainer who travels the UK running training courses for groups of 6-16 people in subjects like Project Management, Time Management, etc.

He also organises training courses for individuals to attend, in the Hampshire / Dorset area, and runs Diploma In Management programmes for groups across the UK.

See www.chriscrofttraining.co.uk for more information, and lots of free stuff.

> Simply pick a topic, like chairing meetings and motivating staff and you'll be taken to a list of handy tips

A t one end of the scale there are spectacular apps that make the most of the iPad's processing power and graphics capabilities. And then there's Mgmt Cards, which sits at the low-tech end of the spectrum. But it's the content that counts, after all, and this app is an excellent *aide-mémoire* for the busy leader in a meeting.

It comprises a set of management-reference cards that were originally designed to support the app developer's own leadership-coaching programme. Now they've been converted to a digital format so you can keep them with you at any time.

Pick one of the topics, such as chairing meetings and motivating staff, and you're taken to a packed list of handy tips, although you can also swipe through the cards. For every obvious tip, such as the advice to "be assertive" in meetings, there's a more illuminating titbit. In the card for organising teams, for example, there's a checklist of the success factors that your team needs to fulfil in order to complete a project.

Given the brevity of the cards' content, this isn't the sort of app that's going to be a lot of use for a new leader who needs a wealth of in-depth information at his fingertips. But if you want a quick way to impress people at a meeting, that conciseness plays into your hands.

By scanning the contents of a card during a meeting, you'll be able to reel off impressive business knowledge, or a pearl of management insight, making it appear like a spontaneous flash of inspiration.

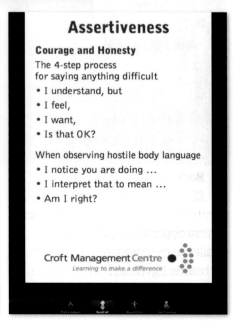

Assertiveness

Courage and Honesty
The 4-step process
for saying anything difficult
• I understand, but
• I feel,
• I want,
• Is that OK?

When observing hostile body language
• I notice you are doing ...
• I interpret that to mean ...
• Am I right?

Croft Management Centre
Learning to make a difference

PUT YOUR FEET UP WITH THE...
5 BEST BOARD GAMES

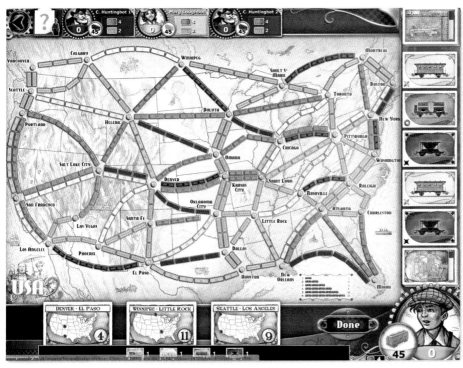

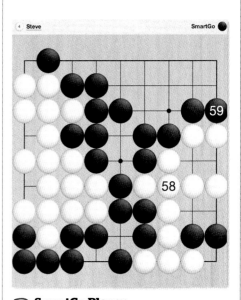

1 Ticket to Ride · £4.99 · bit.ly/ticketgame
This award-winning adaptation of the incredibly successful board game lets you build railways across the USA. If that doesn't provide enough of a challenge, you can buy extra maps for Europe, Switzerland and Asia.

2 SmartGo Player
£1.99 · bit.ly/smartgoipad
The 4,000-year-old Chinese game arrives on the iPad in this stylish version. As an added perk, the computer gives up when it's too far behind (now there's a challenge).

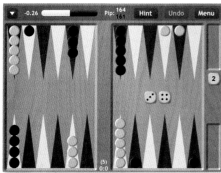

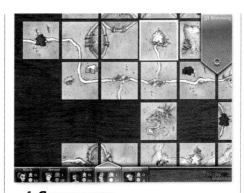

3 Backgammon HD
£1.99 · bit.ly/bgammon
Play turn-based or live backgammon against opponents around the world, or challenge the computer. Choose from six boards: Egyptian, Roman, Medieval, Victorian, Modern or Classic.

4 Carcassonne
£6.99 · bit.ly/carcassonneipad
Play against nine computer opponents, or five real ones, as you build a medieval landscape. There's also an online multiplayer option. Whatever you choose, it'll absorb you for hours.

5 Small World
£4.99 · bit.ly/smallworldipad
Control dwarves, wizards, amazons, giants and orcs as you build an empire, conquering your opponents' territory in the process. Play face-to-face with a friend, or against the computer.

CHAPTER 3
BETTER LEADERSHIP

BEST APP FOR...
BECOMING AN INSPIRATIONAL MANAGER

MindTools HD · Free · bit.ly/mindtoolshdipadapp

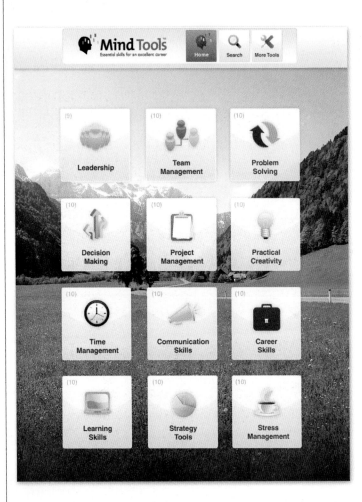

Forming, Storming, Norming and Performing

Helping New Teams Perform Effectively, Quickly

Effective teamwork is essential in today's world, but as you'll know from the teams you have led or belonged to, you can't expect a new team to perform exceptionally from the very outset. Team formation takes time, and usually follows some easily recognizable stages, as the team journeys from being a group of strangers to becoming a united team with a common goal.

Whether your team is a temporary working group or a newly-formed, permanent team, by understanding these stages you will be able to help it quickly become productive.

Understanding the Theory

Psychologist Bruce Tuckman first came up with the memorable phrase "forming, storming, norming and performing" back in 1965. He used it to describe the path to high-performance that most teams follow. Later, he added a fifth stage that he called "adjourning" (and others often call "mourning" – it rhymes better!)

Teams initially go through a **"forming"** stage in which members are positive and polite. Some members are anxious, as they haven't yet worked out exactly what work the team will involve. Others are simply excited about the task ahead. As leader, you play a dominant role at this stage: other members' roles and responsibilities are less clear.

This stage is usually fairly short, and may only last for the single meeting at which people are introduced to one-another. At this stage there may be discussions about how the team will work, which can be frustrating for some members who simply want to get on with the team task.

Soon, reality sets in and your team moves into a **"storming"** phase. Your authority may be challenged as others jockey for position and their roles are clarified. The ways of working start to be defined and, as leader, you must be aware that some members may feel overwhelmed by how much there is to do, or uncomfortable with the approach being used. Some may react by questioning how worthwhile the goal of the team is, and by resisting taking on tasks. This is the stage when many teams fail, and even those that stick with the task may feel that they are on an emotional roller coaster, as they try to focus on the job in hand without the support of established processes or relationships with their colleagues.

Gradually, the team moves into a **"norming"** stage, as a hierarchy is established. Team members come to respect your authority as a leader, and others show leadership in specific areas.

Now that the team members know each other better, they may be socializing together, and they are able

---

I f you're a new manager of a team, a lot will be expected of you. To earn their respect, you'll have to motivate them, and learn how to make tough decisions. MindTools HD, an easy-to-understand collection of management techniques, offers any new team leader all the answers they'll ever need.

Each of its dozen topics, ranging from leadership to stress management, is shown as a chunky button on a 4 x 3 grid. Tapping one brings you to a list of well-written articles about that topic. They're not clichéd re-hashes of the latest theory of people-management either, although general principles, such as 'management by walking around', and the 'GROW' model for achieving goals, are fully covered.

Instead MindTools HD offers practical, often step-by-step, case studies of how to develop and perform a particular skill. In the Team Management section for example, the article on ethical leadership isn't limited to a dry definition of what values you should display. Because solutions to ethical dilemmas aren't always obvious, the article teaches you ways to spot the trigger points of a potential problem and how you can prepare for it in advance.

Each article is neatly suffixed by a summary of its key points and a collection of tips to make you better at the task in question.

As there's so much on offer here, there could be little complaining if you had to pay for the information in this app, as it would still be worth recommending. But the fact that it's completely free moves MindTools HD squarely to the 'must-have' category.

BEST APP FOR...
BRILLIANT BRAINSTORMING

iBrainstorm • Free • bit.ly/ibrainstormipadapp

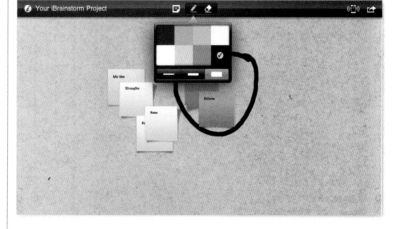

Brainstorming sounds a bit hackneyed these days, though it still sounds better than some of the pretentious management jargon you occasionally hear in the office. But whatever you call it, the concept remains invaluable. Sharing ideas and encouraging your team to engage in the shaping of projects is a vital part of producing great ideas and building a successful team. But if you've ever been in a brainstorming session where colleagues fight over the flipboard, you'll know how pointless some of these sessions can be.

iBrainstorm, the easiest-to-use collaboration tool on the iPad, is a more effective way to share ideas. It lets you quickly add an idea to a pinboard-type background by clicking the '+' button at the top of the screen to add a virtual 'sticky note'. Just double-tap this to bring up a keyboard, then type your idea. Tap back on the pinboard to re-arrange the note by dragging it. You can also bring up a pencil tool to highlight particular notes or draw links between them.

Such tools make organising ideas easy. But as it stands, it still means only one person can be in charge of the iPad at a time. Here's how iBrainstorm solves that: with a quick tap on an icon at the top of the screen, you can find other devices using the app on your local network (Wi-Fi or Bluetooth) so you can collaborate.

Even better, thanks to a free companion app (bit.ly/companionipadapp), colleagues with an iPhone or iPod Touch can also share the screen. Because this makes sharing your ideas so easy, they should flow faster, and you'll find yourself creating little ad-hoc sessions to test how good they are.

BEST APP FOR...
SOLVING LEADERSHIP PROBLEMS

Unstuck • Free • bit.ly/unstuckipadapp

While it's easy to see how an iPad app can help you manage a team, it's tougher to picture it helping you make decisions. But that's just what Unstuck does, and in a unique way.

Unstuck is an app for helping you get through what it calls "stuck moments", whether those are conflicts at work or personal dilemmas. Once you've registered, the app steps you through a fascinating diagnostic approach over a series of beautifully designed screens. First, you describe how you're feeling when you don't know what to do by choosing three cards, each representing an emotion. Then you rank them according to how significant they are. Next, you identify the type of problem – if it's personal or a conflict with someone else.

All the time Unstuck is keeping track of your answers, but by using different techniques to tease out the underlying problem, you get a different perspective on it. You can view and edit your answers at any time by tapping the scrunched-up ball of paper in the corner of the screen.

After a few minutes of questioning comes the diagnosis. Unstuck doesn't offer a specific set of instructions to

solve the problem, but reveals how you're acting – describing you as anything from a "deflated doer" to a "lone leader". On the same page, it also tells you the proportion of other Unstuck users who are feeling a similar way, and more importantly identifies a specific tool to address it. Using this tool you answer a further set of questions based on your earlier revelations and arrive at a solution.

It's intensive work, but the technique is hugely effective, and the tools are tailored to your problems.

By the end of the questions you should have been able to develop an approach to get things moving again.

You'll find yourself turning to this incredibly useful app time and time again when you're struggling with a perplexing work-related dilemma.

Discover MacBook Pro
with Retina display at Square.

It redefines what a notebook can be.

The all-new MacBook Pro features a stunning Retina display with over five million pixels, an ultra-fast all-flash architecture and the latest quad-core Intel processors. All in an incredibly thin and light design.

Visit our blog for daily help, hints and tricks on using Mac OS X. You'll be an expert in no time!
www.squaregroup.co.uk

Visit Square today. We're your local Apple Experts.

Selfridges
400 Oxford Street
London
W1A 1AB

Square @ Wycombe
Eden Shopping Centre
High Wycombe
HP11 2BY

Square @ Derby
21 Iron Gate
Derby
DE1 3GP

Premium Reseller

0800 08 27753 • **www.squaregroup.co.uk**

TM and © 2012 Apple Inc. All rights reserved.

BEST APP FOR...
SPOTTING AND NURTURING TALENT

AskGrapevine HR • Free • bit.ly/askgrapevineipadapp

> This app is a magazine that you can subscribe to from your iPad for free; the printed version costs £20 an issue

How do you recognise talent and encourage it in your staff so they can produce their best work? It's a question that has long troubled the best HR professionals, and has resulted in a small, but burgeoning talent-management industry. The problem is that talent-management resources in the App Store tend towards idealistic business jargon rather than sound advice. AskGrapevine HR is a welcome exception to that rule and an awful lot more besides.

In fact, this app is something of a revelation. It's a magazine that you can subscribe to from your iPad for free; an incredible bargain considering the printed version of the magazine goes for £20 an issue.

But does the content live up to expectation? Definitely. Unlike the plethora of other human resources magazines, this publication focuses on

talent development and management, and in its 60-or-so pages each month you'll find well-written interviews with companies or individuals who have spotted or rewarded talent. These sit alongside features, such as one explaining how to ensure new staff will succeed in a new role. There's also a dedicated 'problem solver' section which, in the latest issue, explains how an organisation can ensure individuals' effective career progression.

While *AskGrapevine* isn't as polished a publication as, say, *The Economist*, its app is easy to navigate

and use. It's also Newsstand-compatible, so if you opt to allow it, you'll be notified when a new issue arrives, and they can be automatically downloaded in the background to be read later.

And the Search tool, which can either search a particular issue or the entire archive of downloaded publications, turns it from something you can browse into a useful searchable resource. It means you can build up a useful library of HR and talent-management advice and information that's always up to date, ready to refer to when you need it.

PUT YOUR FEET UP WITH THE...
5 BEST STRATEGY GAMES

1 Autumn Dynasty • £4.99 • bit.ly/autumngame
Deploy your swordsmen, pikemen, archers, horsemen and catapults wisely to defend the future of the Autumn Empire, as a peasants' revolt threatens to erupt into civil war. A real-time strategy masterpiece that's deep and engrossing.

2 Civilization Revolution
£1.99 • bit.ly/civrevipad
Sid Meier's classic game looks fantastic on the iPad. Choose an historical leader, such as Abraham Lincoln, Cleopatra or Napoleon, then pick one of 16 civilizations to build from scratch.

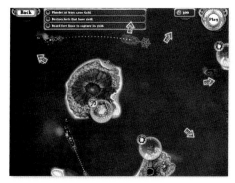

3 Crimson: Steam Pirates
Free • bit.ly/crimsonipad
Command your pirate fleet in the Caribbean in some of the most entertaining missions you'll ever play on the iPad. Capture ships, rescue allies, destroy forts and cause mayhem at sea.

4 TowerMadness
£1.99 • bit.ly/toweripadgame
Over 100 maps will test your tower-defending tactics to the max. There are 17 types of alien, which sounds a lot, but you have 60 powerful weapons to blow them to smithereens.

5 Majesty: The Fantasy Kingdom Sim • £1.99 • bit.ly/majestygame
As the head of a tiny fairytale kingdom, you have to bring prosperity to your people, while fighting enemies and conquering lands. One of the iPad's most sophisticated strategy games.

CHAPTER 4
BE MORE PRODUCTIVE

BEST APP FOR...
ORGANISING YOUR DIARY

Calendars • £4.99 • bit.ly/calendarsipadapp

To say that the built-in Calendar app on the iPad is imperfect is to introduce a new line in understatement. It's clunky, slow, ugly and underpowered. While it works with your iCloud or Outlook-hosted calendars, it syncs awkwardly with Google Calendar – used by many businesses as a collaboration tool.

Calendars (note the extra 's') gives you the best of both words. It will happily include the built-in app's entries, but also syncs directly with Google Calendar, which brings lots of benefits to business professionals.

It looks like its Apple equivalent, and works in a similar way, with five different views: list, day, week, month and year. But editing is much easier – just tap and drag your entries to

re-organise them – and it's a lot faster. It's quicker to flick between months than in Apple's Calendar or the web-based Google Calendar, and you can create new events much more easily in month view just by tapping and holding a day, then entering details of a new event.

But if you like seeing your tasks in a calendar rather than the iPad's

Reminders app, you'll love Calendars for displaying tasks and events in the same window. If you've set up a task in Gmail, it will appear alongside your calendar entries. It's hard not to love the flexibility of reminders. In Apple's Calendar, you just get the option to set a basic reminder, but in Calendars, you can opt to be reminded by email or even a text message, which is fantastically handy for an iPad app, because it can remind you on your phone when your iPad isn't with you.

These might seem like minor improvements to the built-in app. But all those seconds saved and frustrations eased make this worth buying. At just under £5 it's a small price to pay for having all your crucial information at your fingertips.

BEST APP FOR...
ORGANISING MEETINGS

Agendas • £6.99 • bit.ly/agendasipadapp

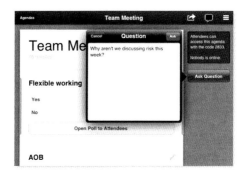

H ere's the way meeting arrangements usually unfold in a big organisation. A prospective agenda is circulated by email. Someone comes back with suggestions for an additional item, which triggers another flurry of emails. Amendments are made and another revised agenda is sent out.

And on the day of the meeting multiple copies of the agenda, minutes and papers are all printed together with extra copies in case anyone has forgotten theirs.

If your business behaves like that, the simple functionality of Agendas could revolutionise your working day. In the app you simply tap an icon to create a new agenda and add text, photos or even polls to each item. Drag items around to reorder them and when you're happy with the shape of the proposed meeting, publish the agenda.

Other people on the same network can then access the agenda by tapping the entry code that you send out. They can respond to polls in the agenda and ask questions from within the app, so there's no need for email. And for those who need a hard copy or

don't have the app on their iPad, you can quickly print or email a PDF of the current agenda to them.

While other users don't have the same privileges as the agenda creator, they can add their own notes by tapping the pencil icon in the top corner of each agenda item, which won't be seen by other participants.

The only thing Agendas doesn't do is let you attach documents. If it did, it would be perfect. But even without that missing option, it's a clear step on the road to the paperless office – and a far quieter email inbox. Which busy executive would argue with that?

> To create a meeting agenda, just tap an icon to create a new one and add text, photos or even polls to each item

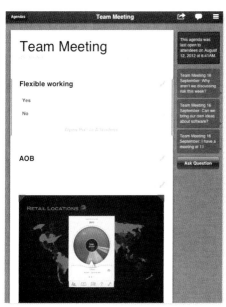

BEST APP FOR...
TAKING AND SHARING NOTES

Evernote • Free • bit.ly/everipadapp

When you're taking notes, and time isn't critical, a simple text editor might be all you need. But in a fast-moving business meeting, you need something as versatile as Evernote.

As a standard text-based note-taker, Evernote is nothing special. You type your notes, organised within notebooks, and append tags to help organise them. But it's the extra features that make this so impressive, in particular the ability to quickly add media to each note. Tap the microphone icon and you can record audio; a godsend if you find your text-based note-taking falling behind

the flow of the conversation. Usefully, when you save the audio, the clips are embedded into the text at the cursor, so when you review your notes, the audio appears in proper context.

Audio will also record in the background even if you switch apps, so if you're taking notes and want to demonstrate something on the iPad, you can do so without losing track of the conversation. You can also add images from the iPad's image library or camera – great for snapping something drawn on a whiteboard, or shown in a presentation.

But the tools for sharing these notes are even better. Because Evernote is an

online service, everything you create on your iPad will be synced to the web and to any Evernote application on your PC or Mac. Importantly, even embedded audio and image files transfer, so you're never without access to your important notes.

You can also share notebooks directly with other Evernote users (they'll see the shared notebook in their Evernote app), and by email or via Facebook, Twitter and LinkedIn.

There are various versions of the app. The basic Evernote account is free, while premium accounts, which give you bigger monthly uploads among other things, start from £2.99.

BEST APP FOR...
CREATING TO-DO LISTS

Wunderlist • Free • bit.ly/wunderlistipadapp

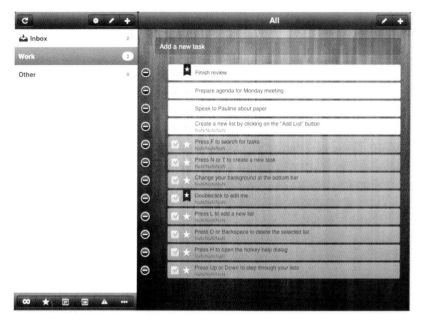

There are loads of task-management apps in the App Store, so many, in fact, that trying to manage them all becomes, ironically, very difficult. Even Apple has tried to get in on the act with its own, limited Reminders app.

But Wunderlist HD is the pick of the bunch as it deals with the two most important things in a to-do app – simplicity and ubiquity – better than the others. It's also free, something that never hurts a business budget.

A task manager needs to be easy to update. Wunderlist HD ticks this box. You add a task by tapping an input field and typing. It then appears as an item in the list below. You can rearrange tasks that you have added by dragging or marking them as completed by swiping them. That's simple enough, but you can also add notes or assign a due date or priority

to each task just by tapping and editing it, which helps ensure that the tasks which need to be done actually get done. Add a reminder and Wunderlist will send you an email when the task is due to be completed. It's not quite a nagging personal assistant, but it's close.

All lists are managed from a small pane on the left of the screen, so you can manage more than one at a time, and separate work from home tasks.

There's no location-based reminder, a feature offered by some rival services. Instead Wunderlist excels in its flexibility. Many rivals sync with iCloud or Dropbox, but Wunderlist offers its own web-based syncing engine, so once signed up you can see and edit your tasks from pretty much anywhere, even if you don't have your iPad with you. That sort of versatility is hugely valuable, meaning you'll never be out of the loop.

Whether at the controls of one of his jets or his many other flying machines, John Travolta daily plays his own role: that of a first-rate pilot who has notched up over 6,000 flight hours and eight certifications on various types of aircraft. That of a man who is passionate about everything embodying the authentic aeronautical spirit. On his wrist is a Breitling Navitimer with its famous aviation slide rule. A cult-watch for all devotees and professionals of the conquest of the skies, equipped with Breitling Caliber 01, probably the best selfwinding chronograph movement. For John Travolta, it is simply the ultimate chronograph legend.

"A MAN PASSIONATE ABOUT AVIATION AND FINE MECHANISMS ONLY SHARES HIS FLIGHTS WITH **THE ULTIMATE CHRONOGRAPH LEGEND**."

BREITLING
1884

INSTRUMENTS FOR PROFESSIONALS™

*RRP. Subject to change without notice.

BEST APP FOR...
EDITING PDFs

PDF Expert • £6.99 • bit.ly/pdfipadapp

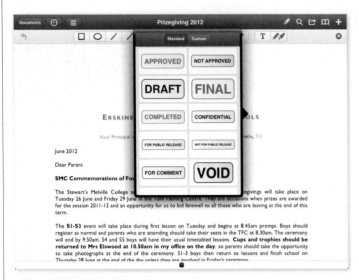

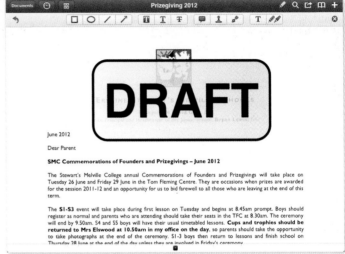

PDF has become something of a *lingua franca* of documents on the iPad thanks to the device's wide support for the file format in its Mail, Mobile Safari and iBooks apps. That's great up to a point because you can be fairly sure that colleagues armed with iPads will be able to open the PDF files you send them. But the fact that you can't do as much with PDFs compared to standard text documents makes the format less useful. That's critical if you want to comment on documents made by someone else or fill in online forms.

But that needn't be the case if you have a tool like PDF Expert, the Swiss Army knife of PDF annotation and editing. Like several other PDF-editing tools, PDF Expert contains an array of document-annotation tools, but it is more impressive as an office-collaboration tool as it lets you add text and apply one of several stamps to documents shared with you.

But where PDF Expert becomes indispensable is when dealing with those ubiquitous PDF forms. There's a text tool to type into form fields, but the app can also capture your signature; and you don't have to scratch your name into a tiny space because – stroke of genius – you're given the whole screen to draw your signature. This is stored and can be added to any subsequent document with a single tap of the screen.

In fact, it's so brilliantly easy to edit documents that you'll find yourself reaching for your iPad, rather than a PC, to edit PDF forms.

You can open Mail attachments or PDFs from other iPad apps, or connect to online storage services, but the simplest way to get files into it is to set your iPad up as a remote drive. You can then simply upload files by connecting to the drive from a PC browser on the same Wi-Fi network.

> It's so easy to edit PDFs that you'll instinctively reach for your iPad rather than a PC to do it

BEST APP FOR...
PLANNING YOUR WORK

Outline+ • £10.49 • bit.ly/outlineipadapp

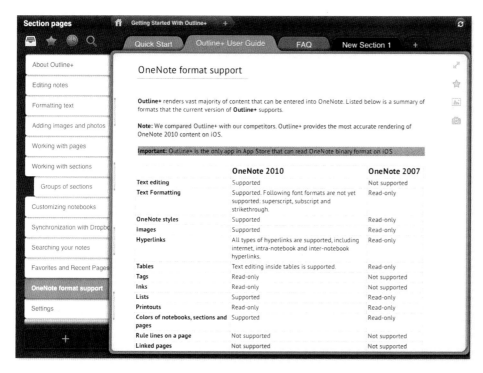

Rush into a task, from writing a report to plotting an in-depth communications strategy, and chances are you'll waste more time later going back to correct things.

It's more productive to structure your thoughts first. Hence the need for an app like Outline+, which is a mixture of note-taker and organiser with fringe benefits. You keep related thoughts in beautiful-looking notebooks, so notes about individual projects can be kept separate. Within a notebook you can type notes anywhere on a page by tapping and holding for a couple of seconds. A text box pops up into which you can type – there's full support for text styling, including bulleted and numbered paragraphs. You can also add images to a page either by importing them

from your image library or taking a picture with the camera.

Whatever element you add, you can rearrange on the page by tapping and dragging, which makes it a great tool for pulling ideas together. There's no limit to the number of pages you can add to the notebook and you simply navigate between them from a list of pages on the left.

The advantage of Outline+ over a physical notebook lies in the way you can organise and retrieve data. You can collate related pages into sections and navigate these from tabs above the page. Outline+ also keeps track of your recently edited pages, which makes it easy to quickly flick back to them. But you can also search for text within a notebook, and between all your notebooks, or mark a page as a

favourite so you can quickly access it later with a few taps of the screen.

Outline+ also synchronises with Dropbox, so your notes are accessible from your PC too. This comes into its own if you're a Microsoft OneNote user as this app reads OneNote files.

BEST APP FOR...
SYNCING ALL YOUR WORK

Dropbox • Free • bit.ly/dropipadapp

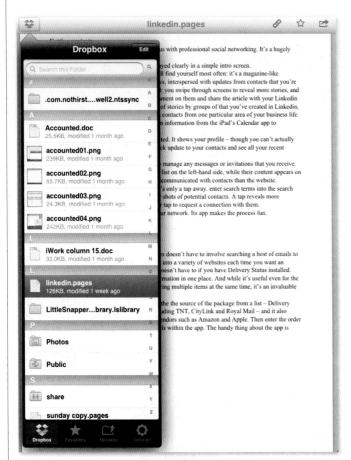

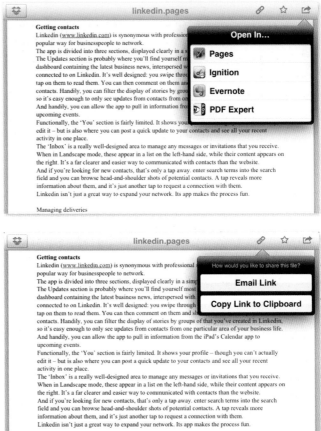

If you're often on the move, your files will probably lie all over the place. While Apple's iCloud is a great way to keep data and files from iCloud-compatible apps like iWork in sync, Dropbox is less restrictive, letting you store files online, and access them in various ways: PC, Mac, the web, and your iPad.

But why is this so useful in business? Well, aside from keeping your files synced, Dropbox offers a great way to share them.

Once you've logged into your Dropbox account on your iPad, you'll see a list of files you've already uploaded to the service (many apps offer direct Dropbox integration too, and you can also upload photos and videos to Dropbox storage from within the app). Dropbox understands what to do with your files. It doesn't have a built-in text editor, but previews documents in a window, and if you tap a button at the top right of the preview window, it can hand over editing chores to other apps.

You can instantly share any file with other people simply by selecting it in Dropbox and then tapping the button to email a link, or to copy it to your iPad's clipboard.

The limited free space (2GB) is less than that offered by rival services such as Google Drive and Microsoft's SkyDrive, but you can nudge this up by referring others to the service. Still, a paid-for team version is affordable at under £500 per year for five users. This allows unlimited storage and the ability to share the same files in a single account.

If you're collaborating, it's easy to revert to previous versions of a document. You can't do this from the app directly, only the website, but it's reassuring to know there's a way to return to earlier versions if needed.

BEST APP FOR...
CREATING FLAWLESS REPORTS

Roambi Flow – Viewer • Free • bit.ly/roambiipadapp

When it comes to internal company reports, most businesses like to keep things conservative. That's why they invariably take the shape of Word or PDF documents. But the important data they contain can be lost in drab diagrams and lengthy explanatory text, and it's often out of date by the time it's produced.

Here's the alternative. Roambi is an online service that lets you transform your raw data into stunning interactive charts. Roambi Flow, a free companion app to this subscription service, displays your reports into fully immersive publications, where the reader can easily interact with the data they are seeing.

How does it work? Well, you create your publication on the Roambi website (www.roambi.com), entering publication details and, using template help, adding images and supporting text. But you can also upload data to the Roambi website because most popular file types are supported, including Excel. You can turn this raw data into impressive visualisations at the touch of a button. When it's all packaged, you can publish the file at your leisure and it'll be instantly available on the Roambi Flow – Viewer app for you to wow colleagues and clients.

All your published documents are kept in the app's library. When you tap the publication, it blossoms into a beautiful magazine-style document, with the text, images and videos

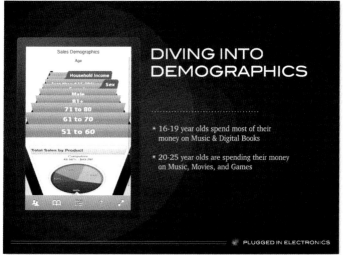

embellished by the interactive charts, which can be tapped and swiped to show more data as and when needed.

It looks great, but more importantly, the report is a lot more engaging than a static publication. And as the Flow app is free to use, all your team can download it and connect to your library of publications. When new editions of the report are available, viewers will automatically be notified so everyone stays up to date.

BEST APP FOR...
MAKING CONFERENCE CALLS

Skype for iPad • Free • bit.ly/skipadapp

If you work from home on your iPad, Skype should be part of your kit. Because the iPad lacks a built-in phone app, Skype, which works over both 3G and Wi-Fi connections, is an inexpensive way of keeping in touch with the office. Calls to other Skype users are free, and calls to standard telephones or mobiles at prices from a little over a penny a minute, are a lot cheaper than calling from the hotel. While some businesses will shell out hundreds of pounds for dedicated hardware teleconferencing equipment, Skype is completely free to use, and often works better.

In some cases, the FaceTime app bundled with recent iPads will do the same thing, but it's hampered by only supporting one-to-one connections, and its calls over 3G may not be allowed by your provider. That missing flexibility is offered by Skype.

When you hold your iPad in landscape mode, contacts appear on the left and messages on the right. It's a couple of quick taps to set up a voice call. Voice call quality is excellent, if inevitably affected by the quality of your internet connection, and you don't need to have Skype running to be notified of incoming calls.

A clever feature of the app is the way you can turn your phone call into a video conference just by tapping the camera icon. It also lets you send text messages to your contacts. However, the current version of this app has one major limitation. While you can use it to participate in a teleconference with

You can turn a phone call into a video conference by tapping the camera icon – and send text messages too

more than one person, you can't actually launch a multi-party teleconference. That means you'll have to rely on someone on a desktop PC adding additional participants for

you either before or during the meeting. But despite that weakness, which should be resolved in an update, Skype for iPad is still the best way of keeping in touch with base.

BEST APP FOR...
PERFORMING COMPLEX CALCULATIONS

PCalc Lite Calculator • Free • bit.ly/pcalcipadapp

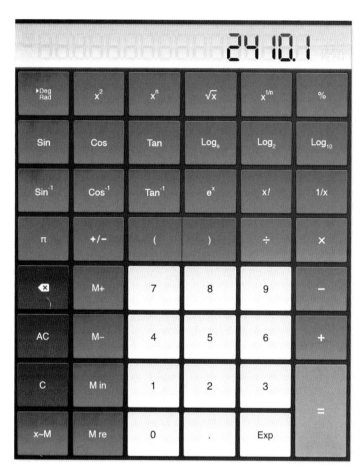

The iPad has a stable of built-in apps, but from a business perspective the one glaring omission is a calculator.

Its absence might be surprising, but it's not critical because a quick browse on the App Store will reveal dozens of free, workmanlike alternatives that you can install. But if you want something that can help run your business, few calculator apps are as powerful – and extensible – as PCalc.

When you hold it in the iPad's portrait mode, PCalc has all the familiarity of a chunky office

calculator, well suited for quickly tapping in a few calculations while you're on the phone. It offers basic calculation functions, plus a few extra functions such as square root buttons, but if you rotate the iPad sideways you gain instant access to a more powerful scientific calculator.

Either way, it's delightfully easy to use. You swipe to the right of the LCD screen to undo an entry or to the left to redo. If you double-tap the display value in the virtual LCD screen you can copy the displayed figure to another app. It couldn't be simpler.

PCalc has some extremely useful extras that you won't find on other apps. A little RPN (Reverse Polish Notation) lets you construct lengthy mathematical expressions without the need for parentheses, while you can easily add mathematical constants to a calculation. The app's most useful button is labelled simply 'A-B'. Pressing this opens a unit-conversions tool for length, speed, volume and weight. More conversions and features are available as in-app purchases, but this free version should offer enough tools for business use.

BEST APP FOR...
FOCUSING AT WORK

Concentrate! • 69p • bit.ly/concipadapp

The downside of having so many fantastic apps to boost your productivity is that unless you're disciplined, they can actually have the opposite effect and distract you. And it isn't only the plethora of iPad apps that can have this effect: traditional business distractions such as phone calls and emails also threaten your productivity every day – let alone the internet. Hence the need for app to help you ignore distractions.

Concentrate is that app. You first choose an amount of time that you want to work for and an amount of time for a break. The attractive pie chart-style display illustrates the passage of time for each. A segment of the chart shrinks as time passes, and its colour changes as it gets closer to completion. When the time you've allocated for work ends, you're prompted to either stop, or continue, when the timer will then track your break period. The process can repeat like this for as long as you want.

Concentrate is prescriptive in how it works. It might irritate some that you can't pause the timer, but it does mean that you're encouraged to stick to the timings you have allocated. And while the app is ideal as a companion for working at a desktop computer, it will also function in the background when you're using the iPad, so while you're using another app, a small notification window appears when the selected time period has passed.

You won't need to use Concentrate if you're a disciplined worker – you'll already manage your time effectively. But for those of us who are aware that their attention can waver, this is an excellent, inexpensive purchase.

BEST APP FOR...
READING WEB ARTICLES OFFLINE

Instapaper • £2.49 • bit.ly/instaipadapp

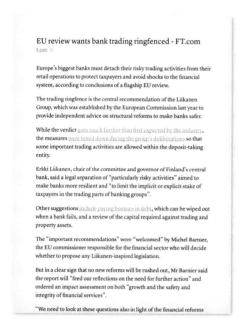

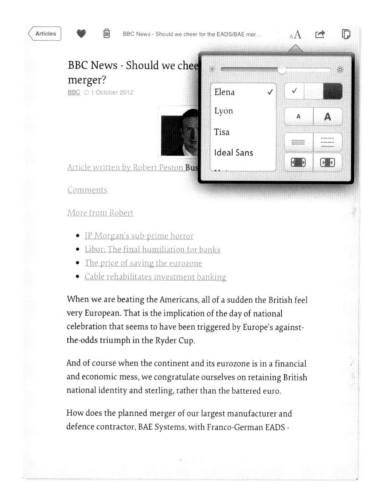

One inevitable dichotomy of business life is this: success demands that you are well briefed, but lack of time means that it's difficult to keep up with important articles that might inform your business decisions. Hence the appeal of apps to store articles for reading offline later, something that may be particularly valuable for owners of Wi-Fi-only iPads that lack a permanent connection to the internet.

Instapaper provides the smoothest way to capture and reformat lengthy web articles for offline use. Once you've set up an Instapaper account online, you can add articles to its reading list from just about anywhere. A JavaScript 'bookmarklet' lets you transfer the contents of the page you're reading from most web browsers – whether on your PC or iPad – to Instapaper, while several other more versatile iPad apps let you send URLs to Instapaper.

When you open the Instapaper app, you can read this synced content minus extraneous information (adverts and so on). All that's left is easily digestible text.

You can customise background and text appearance – fonts, margins and so on. And articles can be sorted into folders, with these changes automatically synced to the server, so you can keep your articles organised the way you want them. Once you've read the article, tap the button at the bottom of the screen to bring up options to delete it, or you can store it in an archive folder.

There are other apps that do similar things. For example, we recommend the free app Pocket if you're capturing lots of links to video rather than text because it displays them better. But Instapaper's text-viewing options are more flexible and its sharing features second to none. A tap takes you to linked articles from your Twitter or Facebook feed, while another features high-quality articles hand-picked by an editor employed by Instapaper.

BEST APP FOR...
HOLDING VIRTUAL MEETINGS

Cisco WebEx Meetings • Free • bit.ly/webexipadapp

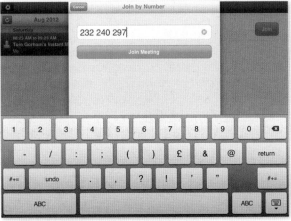

L ogistically, the days of businesses needing to meet in the same room have passed. Virtual-meeting software lets businesses be more productive by allowing people to get together instantly whether they're in the next room or halfway across the world.

The best virtual-meeting software mimics the approach of a traditional meeting. So it is with WebEx. You schedule a time and place for a meeting, invite participants, include an agenda and meeting instructions just as you normally would, and off you go. Logging in to a meeting on an iPad is no more of a hurdle than crossing the office to a meeting room. You enter the meeting number, and password if necessary, then connect. But you can also host a meeting directly from your iPad.

You can share good-quality video from your iPad with other participants. Desktop users can share

their screen with you on your iPad – again the display is crisp – plus particular applications and documents. It's extremely impressive to open a Microsoft Office document on a computer and within seconds see it mirrored on your iPad's screen. All the while you can see and interact with the other participants on screen.

Is complexity the price of such powerful software? Fortunately not. It's easy to control a meeting from

your iPad: you can change which participant is in control of the meeting by tapping and dragging a ball over their name, and you can also launch a private chat with any other participant just by tapping their name.

The best news is that for smaller businesses, all this might be available for nothing. Not only is the app free, but so is a basic subscription to the WebEx service, which lets three people take part in a videoconference.

> Controlling meetings is easy. You can also launch a private chat with any participant by tapping their name

BEST APP FOR...
KEEPING INFORMED

Reeder for iPad · £2.99 · bit.ly/reederipadapp

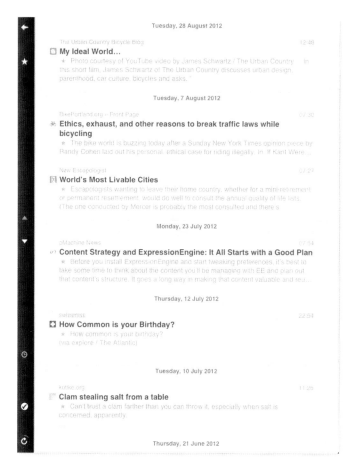

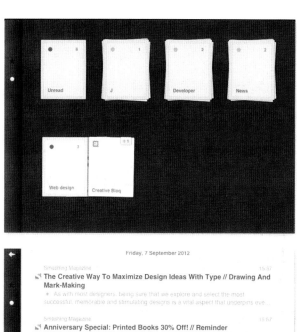

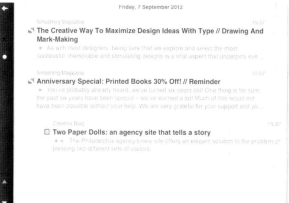

Many business websites offer RSS feeds, which means that equipped with a suitable reader, you can automatically retrieve their latest content without having to load each site in your web browser. Many sites do this using Google Reader, Google's web-based RSS reader, but that prevents you reading articles offline.

Reeder is currently the best way to read RSS feeds on the iPad. It easily syncs with Google Reader and, for simplicity, any articles you've read on the iPad are instantly marked as read on the web-based reader.

But Reeder looks and feels so much better than a web browser. Its dashboard screen organises information neatly by displaying folders containing individual RSS feeds as stacks, while a separate stack contains all unread articles, so you can browse these together. You can pinch a stack to get a quick preview of the news feeds inside, and pinch again to preview all the articles inside that particular news feed.

You tap a stack to open a new window with all its constituent articles. In portrait view, the articles are displayed on the left and, when tapped, their text is shown underneath a headline. You simply tap to show the article in its original web view.

If you're using Reeder as a business tool, it's likely you'll want to store articles for later reference or to share with colleagues or customers. Reeder is well suited to both uses. You can swipe an article to mark it as a favourite and switch the view in an instant to show favourite articles – or to share it to any supported services, such as Twitter and Instapaper.

Reeder has enough features to be easy to use, but still offer lightning-fast syncing – a priceless combination.

BEST APP FOR...
SCANNING DOCUMENTS

DocScan HD Pro • £2.49 • bit.ly/docscanipadapp

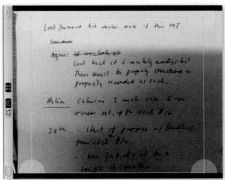

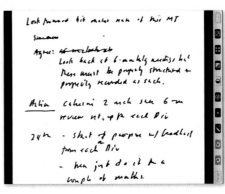

> If you're scanning a page from a book or magazine, DocScan will compensate for 'page curl' distortion

A typical business dilemma: should you invest in a photocopier or stick to a desktop scanner? Well, you could always save money and space by owning neither and using an iPad and DocScan HD instead, which is simpler to use than a photocopier and less hassle than a scanner.

DocScan is flexible because not only will it capture newspaper articles, or meeting notes that you'd like to share with colleagues, but it can also take pictures of anything from business cards to whiteboard scribblings. And its range of export options make it extremely easy to share scans with colleagues.

Its controls are simple: just tap a button and take a picture of the document with the iPad's camera (you can also import a picture from your image library). The picture doesn't have to be pinpoint accurate because you can drag your finger over the resulting preview image to adjust the border guides, which crop the image.

Here, DocScan is unusual in that it can compensate for 'page curl' – perspective distortion – which is handy if you're scanning a page from a thick book or magazine.

The quality of the resulting scan is usually fine for sharing, but you can adjust brightness and contrast for a clearer picture and annotate it to add comments. There's even a black-and-white filter to preview what the scan will look like on a mono printer.

Once you're happy with your adjustments, you can save the scan as a PDF document and store it within the app. This is where its sharing potential shines. The free app lets you share the PDF by email, but this Pro version lets you export to Dropbox, Evernote and other file-hosting services – well worth the asking price.

PUT YOUR FEET UP WITH THE...
5 BEST CASINO GAMES

1 Poker by Zynga • Free • bit.ly/pokeripad
Aimed at Facebook users, Zynga's poker game has over 6 million players worldwide. Chat with your friends online as you play Texas hold 'em, but try not to give anything away. That's never a good tactic – unless you're bluffing.

2 Card Ace: Casino
Free • bit.ly/cardaceipad
Play Texas hold 'em poker, blackjack, slots, roulette and word-game spin-off Word Ace, which is unique to this app. Take on thousands of gamblers worldwide on the public tables.

3 Aw Craps!
£1.49 • bit.ly/crapsipad
Its killer feature is the five-coloured dice which have different probabilities, letting you test betting strategies against different types of shooters: hot, warm, standard, cool and cold.

4 Roulette 3D
£1.49 • bit.ly/rouletteipad
For some enjoyable, risk-free betting, spin these roulette wheels. There are three roulette tables to choose from (American, French and European), and you have 26 'achievements' to unlock.

5 Texas Poker
Free • bit.ly/texaspokeripad
If you're feeling lucky, buy 150 million chips as an in-app purchase (£69.99). If not, just dive in for free and see how you get on. A gambling app that's ideal for experts and novices alike.

CHAPTER 5
BE MORE PERSUASIVE

BEST APP FOR...
BEING MORE ARTICULATE

Word Wit • 69p • bit.ly/wordwitipadapp

If there's one thing that can shatter your credibility among your work colleagues, it's getting words mixed up. If you're the sort of person who has been pulled up over the misuse of 'principal' and 'principle' or someone who doesn't know their apprise from their appraise, Word Wit will be a valuable new ally.

Word Wit offers a way to help you master confusing word pairs – a sister app, Phrase Wit (bit.ly / phrasewitapp) does the same for phrases people often get wrong. Mastering the differences between words is often a chore, but this makes it fun by taking the gaming approach. You spin a spiral to reveal words that are commonly misused next to the word that they are often confused with. Some word pairs might be easy to identify, but others, such as the difference between 'doable' and 'actionable', or 'infer' and 'imply' are more awkward to explain.

Tap one of the words to read its definition and a quote showing how it's used. By tapping a small button you can then test how well you understand the difference between them. Word Wit shows a series of phrases, each with a missing word, and you have to choose which of the word pairs fits. If you pass the test, you're given a key to the Master's Lounge, an area where you can track your progress, and your times for passing each test are recorded. There's also a social aspect to the game: you can see which words are being searched for by other users.

There's little doubt that, boosted by an improved vocabulary and greater eloquence, your persuasive techniques will improve dramatically.

BEST APP FOR...
WINNING EVERY ARGUMENT

Crucial Confrontations • Free • bit.ly/crucialipadapp

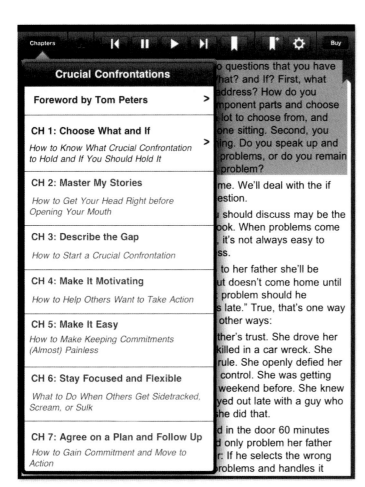

If you need to argue a case, Crucial Conversations will give you lots of techniques to help. It takes the text of the best-selling book and puts it on your iPad, so you can have it with you all the time. It teaches you how to manage tricky discussions, such as asking for a pay rise or dealing with disputes with neighbours, helping you develop valuable persuasion techniques that can have a huge impact on your business and personal life.

It urges you not to jump to a false conclusion when involved in a conflict. Instead, you should identify the correct problem – often this is a tougher task than it might initially appear – and then look at a way to resolve the conflict without apportioning blame.

If you've read an ebook from the iBookstore, you'll be familiar with the navigation techniques used in this app. You can bookmark pages to return to them later, as well as adjust font sizes and use a 'night view' mode that darkens the screen for night-time reading. But this app has the advantage of coming with an audio soundtrack that you can play as you read the text, which is highlighted on the page as it's spoken.

The disappointment is that the app is fairly ugly, and while it's nominally free, you only get one chapter included with the book – you have to buy the rest via in-app purchase for £10.49. That's pricey, but given that the book isn't available in the iBookstore, this is currently the only way to read such a seminal text. It's still worth buying, because the fact is you'll be a much better influencer and negotiator after reading it.

BEST APP FOR...
INFLUENCING PEOPLE

Communication Techniques • £1.49 • bit.ly/commtechniquesipadapp

A bit of charm and a lot of self-confidence can help you influence people, but when you're trying to convince an entire audience, the stakes are higher and your preparation needs to very thorough. This good-looking app is a guide to the different communication techniques you can use.

Don't expect interactive examples or even in-depth content. This app – like one of the principles it encourages – keeps things simple, with tips on how to get the most out of your presentation software, as well as wider communication advice.

The presentation tips veer towards common sense rather than inspirational jargon. But judging by how many times such common-sense advice is wholeheartedly ignored, the app's helpful suggestions to avoid reading the slides while presenting,

choosing fonts wisely and taking time to plan is well worth repeating.

But the app also includes excellent tips on getting your message across to a wider audience – even if you're not standing in front of a set of slides. The most important of these is how to connect to the audience using body language and eye contact, but it also recommends listening to your audience, and even changing your

> Presentation tips veer towards common sense rather than jargon that's purely inspirational

strategy mid-stream, an approach that demands a hefty amount of preparation in advance.

Given the brevity of the content, we wouldn't pay much more than the asking price for this app – but at £1.49 it's hardly going to break the bank. Nevertheless it serves as a good checklist of the things you need to consider when you're asked to communicate to a large group.

BEST APP FOR...
BUILDING RELATIONSHIPS

The Code of Understanding • £1.99 • bit.ly/codeipadapp

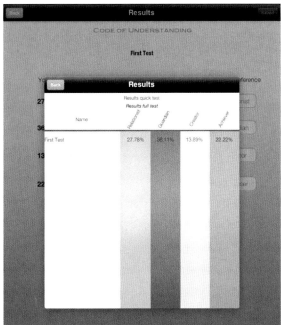

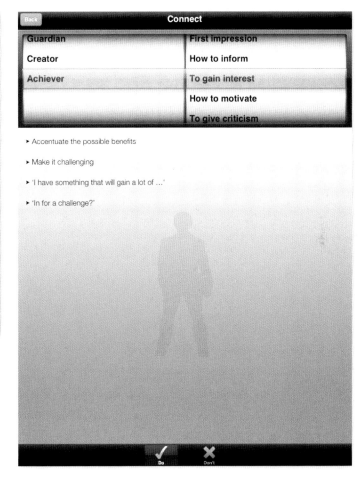

There's no set rule to determine how you communicate with your colleagues, because the best results depend on your team's personalities. What works for one person will backfire on another. So The Code of Understanding tries to identify the best approach to suit your behavioural style, and the way in which your team communicates.

It does this through a series of brisk, easy-to-answer questions. Answer these honestly and the app builds up a picture of your behavioural type, which it divides into one of four categories: relational, guardian, creator or achiever, all of which are explained. But the app doesn't pigeonhole you into one or the other. Instead, it shows you how much your behaviour fits each type, and you can save these results for reference.

The app also helps you determine the behavioural type of others. Because it can't ask them questions, it does this in a slightly less scientific way, by asking you about their clothing, how they greet people and how they act during meetings.

Once you've established their behavioural type you can then put the app to its purpose: determining the best approach to take when communicating with colleagues. To find out how a person will react under certain circumstances, you choose the behavioural type you established

earlier, then pick a situation from a list, and the app will reveal how people are likely to react. The Code of Understanding uses the same technique to offer tips on how to best communicate with a person matching a particular behavioural type, such as techniques to motivate them or engage their interest. Just as importantly, it offers a list of things you *shouldn't* do with certain types.

It's hugely fascinating, and the results the app offers can be illuminating. Try it if you feel you're not getting your point across.

BEST APP FOR...
MASTERING BODY LANGUAGE

iBodyLanguage • 69p • bit.ly/ibodylanguageipadapp

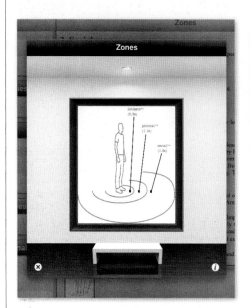

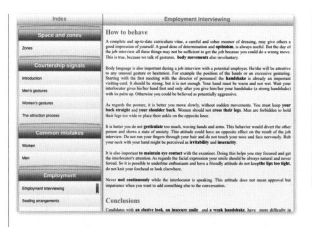

> There are tips on how to trigger a body language signal to determine if someone may be lying

Body language is a hidden language that everyone speaks, but few understand. Yet it's one of the most powerful ways to communicate. Mastering it can be a powerful tool when you need to be at your most persuasive.

An investment of few hours spent studying iBodyLanguage should make you a proficient interpreter of body language during negotiations and team meetings. The app largely reads like a book. In Landscape mode types of body language, such as hand, eye and leg signals, are shown on the left-hand side, together with a fascinating separate section on how to detect lies and an overview of the interpretation of personal space. Tapping one of these categories shows an explanation on the right, revealing in depth the tell-tale signals to look for. There are also tips on how to use questions to trigger a body language

signal: to determine, for example, if somebody may be lying. Illustrations at the bottom of the screen also help you identify the subtle meanings in particular gestures.

Aside from the insight that the app provides into everyday gestures and behaviour, the most useful section in iBodyLanguage is an 'Employment' category. This contains loads of handy

body-language tips that you can use when you negotiate with others. It goes into the detail of the positive persuasion tools and posture you should adopt during an interview, where and how to sit in meetings, and the signals that your boss gives out.

Armed with the knowledge provided by this app, your business meetings will never be the same again.

PUT YOUR FEET UP WITH THE...
5 BEST GOLF GAMES

THE #1 GOLF GAME FRANCHISE
RETURNS WITH NEW FEATURES!

37 YDS
105 YDS
177 YDS
247 YDS

LUSH, HD-QUALITY VISUALS

SCORE 6467
HIGH 271489
80
10MPH

PERFECT SHOT! FULL F

ACCURACY SCORE
3,000

1 Tiger Woods PGA TOUR 12 • Free • bit.ly/tigeripad
The brilliant console game swings onto the iPad in style, with eight courses and a Tiger Challenge featuring 20 mini-games. Easily the most realistic golf game you can play on any platform, and one of the most enjoyable too.

2 Flick Golf Extreme! HD
£1.99 • bit.ly/flickapp
If you thought holes-in-one were hard to get in real life, try achieving them in this game. You find yourself in bizarre locations, with winds strong enough to blow St Andrews to St Lucia.

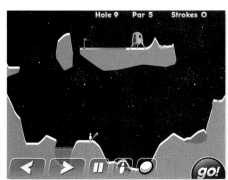

Hole 9   Par 5   Strokes 0

go!

1UP 7,100

HOLE in ONE!

R   01:96

Peter 0 7
Shot 1   Par 3   211 yds   3 MPH

100%
75%

3 Super Stickman Golf
69p • bit.ly/stickmangolf
This turns golf into a crazy physics-based puzzler, letting you do things Rory McIlroy could only dream of (stopping shots in mid-air!). Unlike any golf game you'll have played before.

4 Worms Crazy Golf
£1.99 • bit.ly/wormsgolf
Welcome to the craziest golf, ever. Unleash chaos on the fairway with exploding sheep, ball-stealing moles, irate grannies and suicidal worms. It's not very sensible, but it is very funny.

5 Let's Golf! 3
Free • bit.ly/letsgolfapp
Create an avatar then tee off in places that you won't find on the PGA Tour, such as forests, waterfalls and on the top of skyscrapers. Buy skills to boost your game, then start swinging.

CHAPTER 6
PUBLIC SPEAKING

BEST APP FOR...
CREATING MULTIMEDIA PRESENTATIONS

GoodReader for iPad • £2.99 • bit.ly/goodreadipadapp

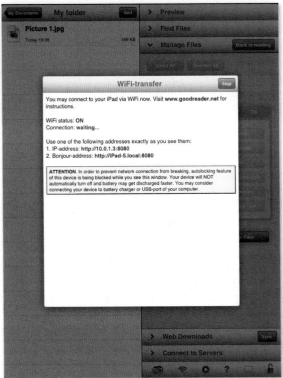

GoodReader was probably never designed as a multimedia presentation app. It just ended up that way. The app's core ability lies in a more prosaic field: opening and viewing huge PDF files and text files. It does this better than any alternative, which is reason enough to add the app to your iPad.

But in fact, GoodReader is multi-functional, which makes it a great presentation tool. Importantly, it hosts dozens of file formats, so as well as PDF and text files it will happily cope with all video and audio formats that the iPad supports. If you're giving a presentation that mixes video footage and image formats, GoodReader holds them all in one place.

It's also an excellent presenter too. Files and folders are collected in a Documents area and you just tap the media files to play them in their own viewer. You can also play a slideshow of all image files in a particular folder.

In terms of multimedia, what sets GoodReader above other presentation tools is the way it automatically synchronises individual files and entire folders through various online folders, whether email servers, Dropbox and SkyDrive online services, or even standard FTP servers. So, in most cases, you never need to worry if the media you're carrying around in GoodReader is up to date.

Even ad-hoc uploading of files is possible from any computer on the same Wi-Fi network: just tap a button and your iPad becomes a sort of file server to which you can upload files via a web browser on the PC.

Even if it doesn't open every file format, all isn't lost. For example, if you need to save a PowerPoint file, you can save it to PDF and sync it to GoodReader. You can even annotate the file inside the app.

BEST APP FOR...
SOUNDING MORE CONFIDENT

A Better Speaker • £2.49 • bit.ly/abetterspeakeripadapp

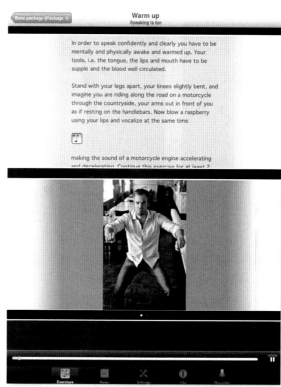

Your voice is more important than you might think. As this series of videos from voiceover artist and vocal coach Jonathan Tilley explains, the way you speak can often be the deciding factor in a job interview or how you come across at a meeting.

A strong voice can also have side benefits. It's likely to raise your self-confidence, which can affect your job performance in other ways.

But the real benefit of a good speaking voice is the ability to stand up and be heard in public. And if you want to improve your performance in this area, install this app. It has 10 exercises, with two more available as in-app purchases, that explain the basics of more assertive speaking. The exercises come in the form of an audio soundtrack that you can use in two ways. You can choose to listen to the whole of each exercise in one go, or use the app more as a book. The screen is split into two, showing the exercise text above supporting images, and there are buttons embedded in the text that you tap to play the audio at the appropriate point.

The lessons you can learn from the exercises are invaluable. They explain the importance of posture in speaking: having your toes pointing outward and maintaining good balance are key.

You'll also learn the important difference between the diaphragmatic and shallow breathing techniques, and why deeper breathing is better if you're speaking in public.

The main rules of pronunciation are covered (albeit inevitably too briefly), as well as how vowels make consonants really sing.

While it's not central to the app, its voice-recording tool is a good way of testing yourself to see how well your pronunciation is improving.

BEST APP FOR...
TELEPROMPTING

Teleprompt+ for iPad • £10.49 • bit.ly/telepromptipadapp

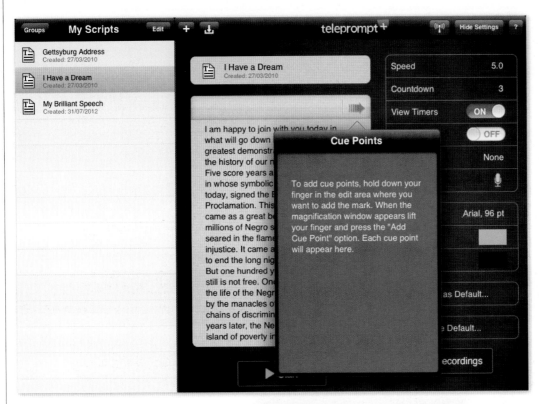

> Because it lets you record videos of your script, this app is just as useful for practising your speech as presenting it

Plenty of speeches and presentations involve reading from a script, but if you're armed with a teleprompter, you don't need to have your head deeply buried in your notes as you present.

Traditional teleprompters cost thousands, though. But Teleprompt+ for the iPad only costs a tenner. The good news is that you don't need to fiddle about too much to get started.

If you want things at their most basic, you simply type your speech directly into the app's main window, then press the start button to start your script scrolling down the screen in large type, making it easy to read.

But it's the way you can tweak things that sets this app apart. You can adjust how fast the text scrolls (even adjusting its speed while presenting by dragging the text on screen), and also organise scripts into groups and import them directly from online services such as Google Docs and Dropbox – which means your team can be finessing your script up to the last minute. Because it lets you record videos of your script, it's just as useful for practising your speech as presenting it. There are other neat extras, including cue points that can be embedded in the script to make them easy to jump to if you need to adjust your speech as you give it.

It's amazing that an app at this price has so many high-end features. These include text mirroring, so the script can be seen on the glass reflectors that are often found at large venues. With the addition of a suitable adapter, you can link up your iPad to a big screen to display the text. There's even Bluetooth support for hands-free control of the teleprompter as well as all sorts of add-on controllers – from iPhone to foot controllers.

BEST APP FOR...
DISPLAYING WHITEBOARD NOTES

Educreations Interactive Whiteboard • Free • bit.ly/educreationsipadapp

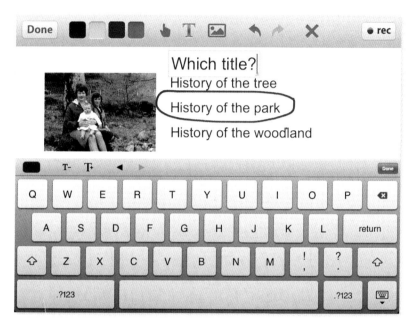

Whiteboarding – drawing on an interactive board – is an established way to gather ideas together during a creative meeting. But afterwards, the results can be awkward to collate. This simple app puts that whiteboard interactivity on your iPad, which means no more fruitless searching for a working marker pen.

The basics are intuitive, if little more than standard fare. You can draw freehand on the screen in one of five colours or use the type tool to add text to the page. You can add images from all sorts of sources, including the iPad's image library; its camera; any image file on Dropbox; and even directly from a web page.

You're not restricted to a single page for your whiteboarding. In fact, you can annotate numerous pages to make a whole deck. And this is where

Interactive Whiteboard gets clever: once your thoughts are in order, press the big record button to record the screen, adding an audio track as you step through the whiteboard.

You can also annotate as you record, even switching between individual pages, and upload the resulting video to the Educreations website (www.educreations.com) where you can share it with colleagues. Critically, you can set

controls so that only people you choose are allowed to watch the video. Given that sharing the results of a whiteboard session can be extremely complicated, this is a fantastic feature. And because you can annotate a recording you can also use it as a basic product-demonstration tool. The only flaw is that you can't store the video on your iPad or export to another service. Still, given that you're getting this all for free, it's a minor gripe.

BEST APP FOR...
PLAYING POWERPOINT SLIDES

SlideShark • Free • bit.ly/slidesharkipadapp

Apple's Keynote app is a great presentation tool. But if you work with PowerPoint, which doesn't have a native iPad app of its own, SlideShark may be a more compatible alternative.

SlideShark isn't just an app; it's an entire online service to which you can upload PowerPoint files from your PC and iPad. You can also use the SlideShark app to download and present them on your iPad.

For those who've had to perform workarounds, such as exporting slides to PDF and presenting PowerPoint slides on an iPad, being able to perform this task is impressive enough on its own. And most presentations transfer to SlideShark seamlessly; it only objects to more complicated ones with transitions or embedded videos or audio.

But there are two things that make SlideShark the best PowerPoint app. First: how comfortably it works on the iPad. You can organise downloaded presentations in a central window, tapping a button to play the one you want. The presentations themselves are easy to control with a finger: drag one way to advance, the other to go back, or drag up to see a thumbnail view of all slides.

SlideShark also supports a presenter view, complete with notes and timer, and there's a lovely pointer mode to focus audience attention that seems made for mobile use: when you're playing the presentation, tap and hold the screen and as you drag

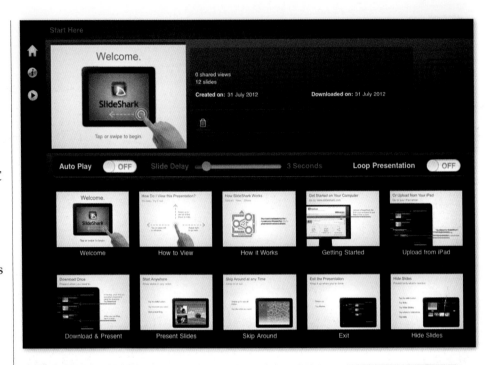

Download Once
Present when you need to.

When you see **Play**, tap it to begin.

Key features include a presenter view, notes, a timer and a pointer mode that's ideally suited for mobile use

your finger across the slide a matching pointer appears.

SlideShark's other essential feature is its ability to show unattended presentations: you can set slides to automatically play and loop. Its weakness is that you can't edit slide content, but some customisation is

possible – you can omit particular slides from a presentation by hiding them. And as it's a hosted service, it's easy to share presentations online.

SlideShark subscriptions come in several flavours, but the free version gives a generous 100MB of space; enough for a few hefty presentations.

BEST APP FOR...
DISCOVERING BRILLIANT QUOTES

Quotes# • 69p • bit.ly/quotesipadapp

Famous Quotes

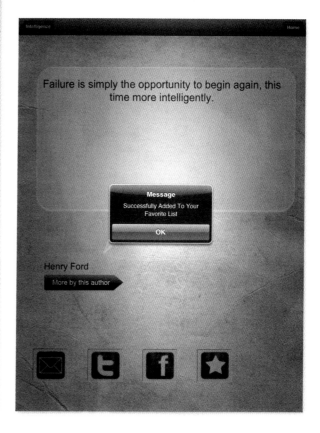

There's nothing like a powerful quote to add a bit of gravitas or humour to a presentation. But finding the right one can take the sort of time that would be better spent honing other aspects of your pitch. That's where iPad-based references come in handiest. And Quotes# offers a quick way to grab the right words.

At first glance, Quotes# doesn't appear to be anything special. Its quirky name and drab background doesn't inspire confidence. And it's limited too: it doesn't let you add quotes of your own (Lickability's Quotebook is the app for that: bit.ly/quotebookapp, £1.99). But you should definitely persevere, because with a whopping 75,000 quotes to choose from, you're guaranteed to find plenty of razor-sharp soundbites to suit your needs.

Because the app doesn't have a search tool, the best way to browse the quotes is by category – there's a fairly lengthy choice including leadership, success and so on. When you select a category, a list of related quotes appears which you can browse by scrolling. Tapping a quote reveals it on its own page, and you can share it by email or social media, or flag it as a favourite. This adds it to a Favourites list which you can access directly from the Home screen.

Quotes# is an app to stick inside a folder on your iPad. It's not something you're likely to use every day, but if you do, you'll probably enjoy the random quote feature. Instead, just open it when you need a great quote and you won't be disappointed.

BEST APP FOR...
PRACTISING AT HOME

Presenter Pro for iPad • Free • bit.ly/presenteripadapp

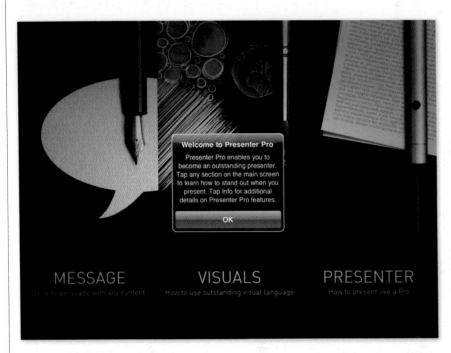

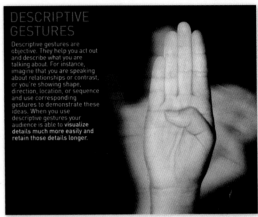

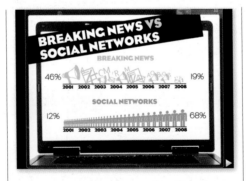

You need more than swish software and technological gimmickry for a great presentation. Instead, its success largely rests on your own shoulders. But technology can still lend a hand. Presenter Pro offers a way to improve how you get your message across.

Its assistance is divided into three broad categories. In the 'A Message' section you can learn how to prepare for your presentation, from the basics of planning and structuring what you're going to say, to practical aspects of defining your audience, and scripting the words you'll deliver.

The ideas shown may sometimes amount to common sense, but they are frequently forgotten by aspiring presenters. One gem encourages you to focus on one main point, rather than addressing several different ideas; another encourages the use of stories to help make your presentation more memorable.

The Visuals section is about how presentation looks: how to best organise its layout and content for maximum impact. There are helpful real-world examples to show the difference a visual rethink can make.

It all comes together in the Presenter section, which helps turn a speech into a performance. Here, topics cover the effectiveness of gestures and being yourself.

Throughout, the advice is shown on beautifully designed slides, which you move between by dragging your finger across the screen. You can switch between sections from a bar that appears when you tap the screen. This easy navigation, coupled with the short and snappy lessons, means this advice isn't the sort of thing you'll scan once and forget. You'll find yourself quickly skipping through this the evening before your presentation.

The app is free, but you'll need to fork out an extra £1.99 as an in-app purchase for most of the features. Even though this should have been made more obvious, it wouldn't have changed our recommendation. This is still an invaluable app for boosting anyone's presentation skills.

PUT YOUR FEET UP WITH THE...
5 BEST BRAIN-TEASER GAMES

1 Big Bad Sudoku Book 3 · 69p · bit.ly/sudokuipad
The best thing about this Sudoku game is that the leaderboard is on Apple's Game Center, so you can show off your skills to the world. Challenge mode has 50 puzzles.

2 World of Goo HD · £2.99 · bit.ly/gooipad
Drag and drop living Goo Balls to build bridges, cannonballs, zeppelins, and giant tongues. Sounds bonkers, but five minutes playing it and you'll be hooked.

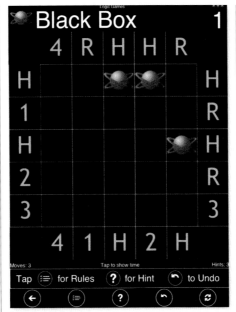

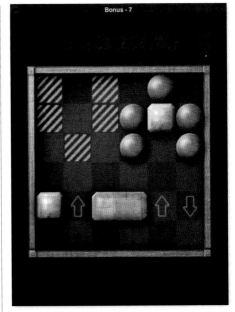

3 Unblock Me
Free · bit.ly/unblockmeipad
To exercise your brain on the journey into work, try to move the red block off the board by sliding others out the way. There are 4,200 puzzles to play.

4 70 Logic Games
Free · bit.ly/logicipad
This compendium includes Calcudoku, a maths sudoku, and Slitherlink - a looping version of Minesweeper. With 1,881 levels to solve, you won't get bored.

5 Escapology
69p · bit.ly/escapeipad
This sliding-puzzle game, where you have to roll wooden balls into position, looks simple - but you have to carefully plan all your moves in advance.

CHAPTER 7
MAKE BUSINESS TRAVEL BETTER

BEST APP FOR...
ORGANISING TRAVEL

Kayak Pro • 69p • bit.ly/kayakipadapp

The maxim that 'the journey itself is the reward' surely doesn't apply to the hassle of business travel. If you don't have someone in your office organising things, arranging flights, accommodation and a decent hotel can take time that would be better spent preparing for your meetings.

Think of Kayak Pro as the next best thing to a personal assistant. Its all-in-one service helps find the best flights, hotels and car rental cars for your business trip.

Let's say you're looking for an urgent flight to Europe. You type your destination and departure dates (as a timesaver you can ask Kayak to use your current location) and the app will search a huge database of online flight providers to display matching results, which you can filter not only by price, but also duration and time of departure. One tap on your chosen selection and you're taken to the relevant website where you can book the flight directly. You can take the same approach for hotel rooms and car rental, which can be filtered by rating as well as price.

It's here that Kayak's 'Autofill' feature comes in handy. Using this, you can enter your name and address within the app, which will be automatically re-entered when you visit any website from Kayak. Over time, this saves a lot of retyping.

Kayak's helpfulness doesn't end there. It saves searches so you can return to them later, but, even better, it stores details of entire trips to its online database. To do so, you simply forward any booking confirmations to a Kayak email address, and by tapping the Trip button on the Kayak iPad app you can pull up these details – neatly organised to show flight number and time. You can also store your own travel notes: a great way to keep all your travel info in one place.

BEST APP FOR...
CONNECTING TO YOUR PC REMOTELY

Ignition • £89.99 • bit.ly/ignitionipadapp

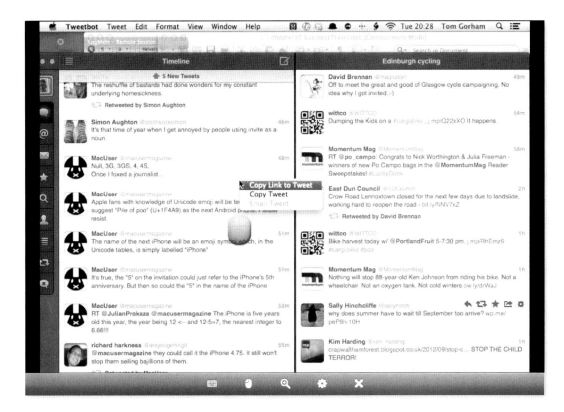

> The superb file manager uses a file-browser view that makes it far easier when you're moving and copying files

The sheer portability of the iPad means it's tempting to forego the additional bulk of a laptop when you're on your travels. But what if you need access to software that's only on your PC? One answer is to install remote-access software, which lets you control and view a remote PC's screen from your iPad.

While there are plenty of alternatives to choose from, including free options, LogMeIn's Ignition app is a reliable and speedy way to connect to your office PC. If you've ever used remote-access software that couldn't punch its way through an office firewall, never mind a paper bag, you'll love the fact that in most cases you can set Ignition up in a

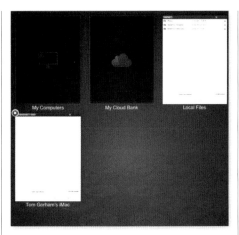

couple of minutes. Often all it needs is a few seconds spent setting up an account on LogMeIn's website (www.logmein.com) and installing the free host software on the computers you'll be connecting to. Then it's

simply a matter of entering your LogMeIn account details on the iPad app and connecting.

There are two ways to use Ignition. The standard route is to use your fingers to mimic the mouse to control the remote screen. In most cases you're better off using Ignition's superb file manager, something lacking in most remote-access software. This swaps the laggy desktop view for a file-browser view that makes it much easier to deal with individual files. Through tapping and scrolling you can move files between your iPad, your remote computer and cloud-storage services such as Dropbox and Google Drive. It's the best way to get vital files quickly.

BEST APP FOR...
TRANSLATING DOCUMENTS

Google Translate • Free • bit.ly/gtranslateipadapp

A second language is always a handy attribute on foreign business trips, but a translation app on your iPad is arguably the next best thing. And when it's free, like Google Translate, it's a no-brainer to add this to your travel arsenal.

You can translate in two ways. The most obvious route is to type the text you want to be translated, then tap the 'Go' button. Google translates text between 57 languages, which you can select at the top of the screen. Alternatively, you can tap the microphone button at the side and dictate what you want translated into the iPad's tiny microphone.

In either case, the translation appears in the selected language in the area below, and, for many of the translations, you can tap a button that speaks the translation for you.

Handily, if you're just translating a single word, Translate will offer a bilingual dictionary definition.

Google Translate won't convert entire documents in one go, but you can paste text from documents you want translated into it, and its translation engine should cope fine with text up to 1,500 characters, or around 300 words at a time.

Google Translate normally needs an internet connection to function, something that might not always be available if you're abroad. But with a bit of advance planning, all may not be lost because translations previously marked as favourites on your iPad are available to access at any time.

Also, Translate keeps your recent translations in its history, the contents of which are also available offline.

Most important of all, Google's results are both fast and reasonably accurate. You might not pick up a job as a translator with the results, but they should be good enough to let you navigate a business meeting or book a taxi to the airport.

BEST APP FOR...
CONVERTING CURRENCY

Currency • Free • bit.ly/currencyipadapp

There are lots of fancy currency-conversion apps in the App Store, but none make it as easy to deal with the exchange rate as this app. Converting currency is a simple two-stage process. You first choose the currency to convert from: the app organises them by continent and then alphabetically by country; in total around 180 are covered.

If you're so totally jet-lagged that you can't remember the country the currency belongs to, you can select it from a map instead. As soon as you select the currency to convert from with a tap, it's set as the base one.

The second stage is to tap the 'change amount' button. Enter the amount you want to convert and tap the Convert button. All the other currencies shown on the screen will then update to show the equivalent amount in their local currency. You can switch between base currencies just by tapping another currency and entering an amount.

This currency-conversion tool is a handy way to avoid expensive mistakes while you're on a business trip abroad, but if your business regularly deals with foreign suppliers or customers, you'll probably use the app in another way: to work out the latest exchange rates with the countries you do business with.

Here's how to do it: add currencies you regularly convert to a Favourites list, and set your base currency. You then set its conversion amount to '1', and all the other currencies will display the current exchange rate. It's a good way to get an at-a-glance picture of its relative health.

Out-of-date statistics are a thing of the past: you can choose to update rates every time you launch the app and also schedule it to update at hourly to weekly periods.

BEST APP FOR...
TRACKING EXPENSES

XpenseTracker • £2.99 • bit.ly/expenseipadapp

Take a photo of your receipts and easily attach any supporting files to your claims

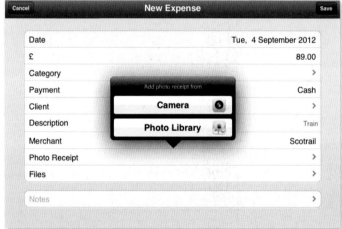

Aside from jetlag or hotel food, the most tiresome part of any business trip is keeping your expense claims receipts together. Even when you're recording your expenditure electronically, it can be a hassle to keep your records up to date. But XpenseTracker takes much of the pain out of recording expenses. Its logical organisation keeps all your expenses from one trip in a log. As well as the overall details about the trip – its start and end date and so on – each log can allocate a *per diem* amount if one has been allocated.

Expense items can be either labelled standard expenses or mileage amounts. In both cases, the process for recording them is the same, but while there are a lot of individual fields that you can complete, these can be hidden, so if you don't want to enter a category for a receipt, you don't have to. And you can add clients (and suppliers) to a central list, which helps if you often submit claims.

You don't need to worry about bits of paper either. XpenseTracker can take a snapshot of your receipts (either from the iPad's built-in camera or

from the Photo Library), and you can easily attach supporting files. Open the built-in Mail app, then tap and hold an attachment to open it in XpenseTracker, from where you can link it to an expense.

There are several ways to get your expenses out of the app, such as exporting them by email as an attachment or through cloud services.

You can export expenses as a spreadsheet or PDF, and customise them to only include particular fields or order them by date. Now there's no excuse to leave them piling up.

THE WEEK
for iPad

DOWNLOAD TODAY!

Experience reading the magazine in this exciting format!

"I rate this as one of the best magazine apps available for download!"

"Perfect format for this elegant digest of the week's key press issues."

"This app is superb."

★★★★⯪

Average iTunes customer review

Daily briefing
The 10 most important news stories brought to you every day

Night mode
Reading in bed? You may find it easier with our special night mode

Read it your way
Adjust the text size or tap straight to your favourite section

Get the picture
Enjoy each image in detail with our full screen view

To get 6 issues FREE, visit
app.theweek.co.uk

BEST APP FOR...
CATCHING FLIGHTS

FlightBoard Pro • £2.49 • bit.ly/flightboardipadapp

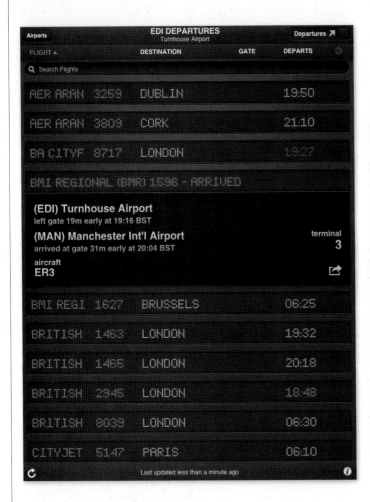

I t's all too easy for the best-laid business travel plans to go awry, particularly if your flight involves multiple connections. While you can watch your plans disintegrate from the departures board at your airport, how can you see the latest flight information if your taxi to the airport is stuck in traffic? And how do you know if the connection you're hoping to catch is still on time?

One answer is to scour airport websites to find out what's happening. Instead, install this handy app, which provides arrival and departure times, updated every five minutes, from thousands of airports, as well as gate information for flights.

FlightBoard's beautiful information display – it's modelled on the flight board of Charles de Gaulle airport – makes it easy to find the details you need. Tap the Airports button at the bottom of the screen, and start entering the name of an airport and the app presents the results immediately, showing flight number, destination and departure gate and time. You can tap any of these column headings to sort information by that category, but you can use the search field above to quickly narrow the results. If you want to warn a colleague about a delayed or cancelled flight, you can email details from the app, or post to Twitter and Facebook.

Inevitably, the app is a hostage to the accuracy of the information provided by the airports, but even taking that into account, you're likely to find FlightBoard priceless as a way to spot potential travel problems. The early warning it provides means you can make changes to your itinerary before your competition does.

PUT YOUR FEET UP WITH THE...
5 BEST WORD GAMES

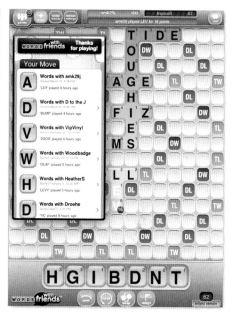

1 WordsWorth HD · £1.99 · bit.ly/wordsworthipad
If you excel in this addictive letter-linking, Boggle-style game, you can join the power players in the WordsWorth Club. If not, you'll be stuck with the rest in the Practice Club. What you need is 12 letters long and starts with a 'p' (perseverance).

2 Words With Friends HD
£1.99 · bit.ly/wwfipad
If you like Words With Friends, but hate the adverts that keep popping up, simply pay to stop them appearing in this brilliant HD version. Play up to 20 simultaneous games online.

3 NYTimes Crossword
Free · bit.ly/cwordipad
For a new crossword challenge, try those set by the *New York Times*, which gives you a free week-long trial. This app has an archive of 6,000 to get through, so you'd better get started.

4 Word Solitaire HD
Free · bit.ly/wordipad
There are loads of conventional solitaire-style iPad games, but this one adds a clever twist by using letters instead of playing cards. Drag them onto each other to make new words.

5 Word Jewels XL
Free · bit.ly/jewelsipad
Word Jewels boasts that it will accept 264,097 words, which must've taken them a while to count. It's another fun word-building app, with no annoying timer to put you under pressure.

CHAPTER 8
START YOUR OWN BUSINESS

BEST APP FOR...
GETTING STARTED

How to Start a Business • Free • bit.ly/howtostartipadapp

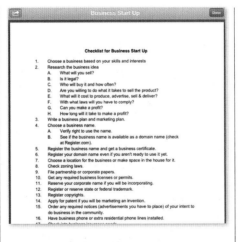

You've got the big idea, but how do you actually get it off the ground? This app from Docstoc (www.docstoc.com) is a great guide to turning ideas into a practical business. It comprises five sections covering the vital components of a start-up, from generating a killer idea and checking whether it's something that will support a business, to how you market it to the public.

Each chapter contains videos presented by successful US entrepreneurs. Throughout, there's authoritative, common-sense advice to all business owners, but the videos don't shirk the difficult stuff, either. A few minutes are spent discussing the thorny topics of accurately pricing your product or service, and avoiding the common mistake of underestimating your own costs.

If it's a little surprising that all this great advice is available for nothing, the explanation is that the app's developer makes its money through editable template documents and downloadable resources that can be bought from its website. But there's no hard sell within the app: you can see full PDF versions of a selection of the most relevant documents from within it, and store these on your iPad or email them directly from the app.

Some, such as the excellent industry-analysis checklist, are a great way to inspire you to start thinking about the most important goals your business will need to achieve to succeed. There's bound to be something you hadn't considered.

If you're thinking of downloading a template, don't lose a moment worrying that it won't be suitable for a UK audience. Docstoc's US origins are sometimes apparent from the video content, but there are British versions of many popular templates too.

This app shouldn't be the only tool in your start-up arsenal, but any existing or aspiring business owner could learn a thing or two from the wealth of sage advice it provides.

BEST APP FOR...
CREATING A BUSINESS PLAN

StratPad: Strategic Business Plan Strategy · Free · bit.ly/stratpadipadapp

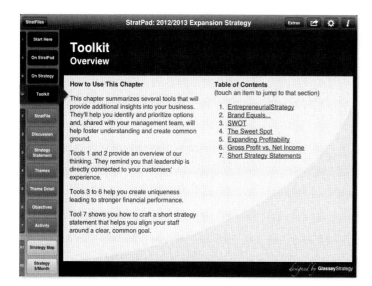

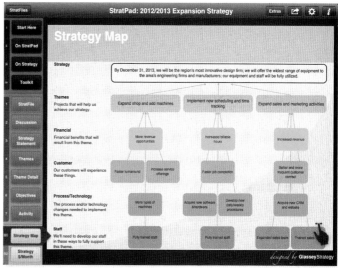

StratPad offers indispensable advice to help you devise a smart plan on how your business will make money. First, the app takes you through an explanation of what a strategy entails. It starts off with the fuzzy stuff – explaining how companies need "soul" – but goes on to explain how any strategy must link to execution: in other words, it explains what you actually *need to do*. There's a useful overview, for example, of metrics and targets, while a toolkit section (not available in the free version) discusses the weapons you can use for insights into your business, including SWOT analysis to analyse the strengths, weaknesses, opportunities and threats it faces.

After the theory, the practice: create a step-by-step business plan by entering it into a StratFile. What you enter here goes from an overall strategy statement to the details: the projects or activities that serve the

strategy, and the dates and financial considerations that underpin it.

In the free edition, you can only enter limited information. You just get a set of template answers from an imaginary company. But these are useful in their own right, because they let you see how specific activities feed into a strategic overview. Only in the more expensive versions of the app, available as in-app purchases, can you enter and edit your own strategy

> StratPad lets you gather your strategy and processes into a map to see how they interact

information. The most expensive edition (£27.99) also lets you export financial projections to a spreadsheet.

If you respond more to visuals, StratPad lets you gather your strategy and processes into a map layout so you can see how they interact. And it uses your data to project a month-by-month strategic financial analysis over the first year. That kind of detail will impress bank managers and help get your business off the ground.

BEST APP FOR...
ATTRACTING VENTURE CAPITAL

Capital Sources for Your Business • Free • bit.ly/capitalsourcesipadapp

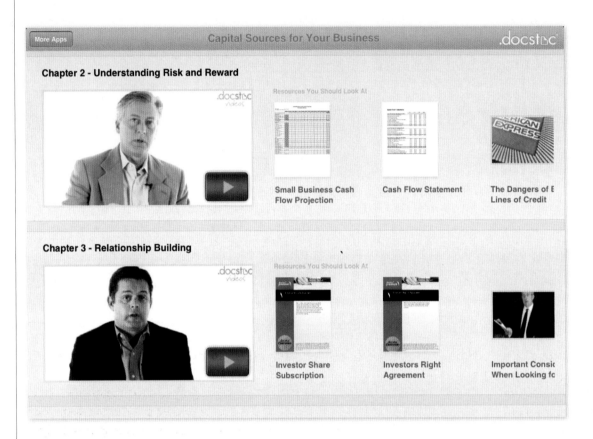

> Short video interviews offer clear explanations of business concepts like risk and reward

A pressing worry of any start-up is how to keep the money flowing during the volatile early years. Irrespective of how good your business idea is, unless you're blessed with a financial cushion provided by a windfall or an uncharacteristically understanding bank, it's likely that you'll burn through your available cash long before you get your idea to market.

Venture capital is often an attractive, if little understood, funding option for entrepreneurs. Essentially, it means that in return for a share in the company, investors will often put up some of their own capital to get the business up and running.

But how do you find venture capital, what are investors looking for – and how do you make sure you don't get exploited in the process? Capital Sources for Your Business is a clever way to understand the benefits and pitfalls of venture capital compared to other sources of income.

The bulk of this app, which comes from the same developer as 'How to Start a Business' (see page 86), comprises a collection of short, punchy video interviews which offer clear explanations of concepts such as the differing types of investment, risk and reward, and so on. There are also tutorials on the less quantifiable aspects of building a business, like

relationship building. It's very persuasive and waffle-free, delivered by knowledgeable venture capitalists and experienced investors.

Alongside these videos are plenty of brilliant resources, from a helpful list of common start-up mistakes to practical example documents, including a cash-flow projection template, and a list of the pros and cons of loans and self funding. You'll need to pay to download editable versions, but you can view and save these PDF versions for free.

This app won't help you run your small business, but you'll be more informed about how to fund it after taking time to explore its content.

BEST APP FOR...
MANAGING YOUR FINANCES

Xero • Free • bit.ly/xeroipadapp

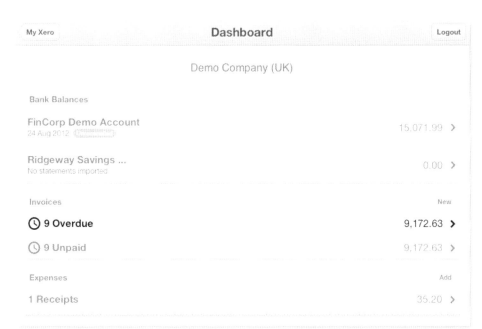

When it comes to running your business's finances on your iPad, you have two options. The first is to use an app that keeps your accounts on your iPad – Easy Books (free, but with in-app purchases, www.easybooksapp.com) is well worth investigating.

But the advantages of using a secure online service are clear. If you lose your iPad, your data is still accessible, and you can access it wherever you have an internet connection. And when an online service has a good supporting iPad app, it's a no-brainer. Xero is one of the best online accounting services for small businesses in the UK, and the only one with a dedicated iPad app.

The app is far simpler than the web-based service. On the iPad you can't generate reports or run bank reconciliations to check the transactions you've entered against your bank statement, but that doesn't matter if you're a busy person on the move, and simply need an oversight of the business's vital stats, and the ability to quickly add expenses and invoices. That's exactly what Xero does – and it does so brilliantly.

Though Xero's online data is securely protected, you can keep your log-in as simple as typing a four-digit passcode, so you can always access your data quickly. Xero's dashboard window shows your current bank balance and any overdue or unpaid invoices, while from a menu located at the bottom of the screen you can switch between contacts, invoices and expenses with a single tap.

You can create and send invoices directly from your iPad with just a couple of taps, and track expenses, literally, in a snap: take a photo of the receipt with your iPad's camera and it will be uploaded to Xero's servers, alongside other invoice details.

If you're after a quick and secure way to manage your expenses on the move, then this is the app for you.

BEST APP FOR...
INCREASING YOUR CONTACTS

LinkedIn • Free • bit.ly/linkedinipadapp

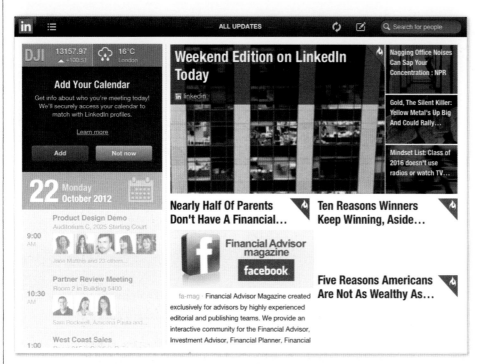

LinkedIn (www.linkedin.com) is synonymous with professional social networking, and is a popular way for businesspeople to increase their contacts. But its iPad app is better looking than the website and far easier to use.

It's divided into three sections. The Updates section is probably where you'll find yourself most often: it's a magazine-like dashboard containing the latest business news, interspersed with updates from your contacts. It's well designed: you swipe through screens to reveal more stories, tapping them to read in more detail.

You can then comment on the stories and share them with your contacts. Handily, you can filter the display of updates to show only those from particular groups you've created

in LinkedIn, so it's easy to only see updates from contacts from one particular area of your business life. Also, you can let LinkedIn pull in information on upcoming events from the iPad's Calendar app.

Functionally, the 'You' section is more limited as, although it shows your profile, you can't edit it. But from here you can post updates and see all your recent activity in one place.

The 'Inbox' section is a well-designed area, from where you can manage messages and invitations. When you hold the iPad in landscape mode, these appear in a list on the left-hand side, while their content appears on the right. It's a far clearer and easier way to communicate with contacts than using the website.

And if you're looking for new contacts – and all new businesses are – that's only a tap away. Enter terms into the search field and you can browse head-and-shoulder shots of potential contacts. A tap reveals more information and another requests a connection with them.

LinkedIn isn't just a great way to expand your network of business contacts; this app makes the process fun and it's simpler to use than ever.

BEST APP FOR...
SETTING UP MOBILE PAYMENTS

mPowa • Free • bit.ly/mpowaipadapp

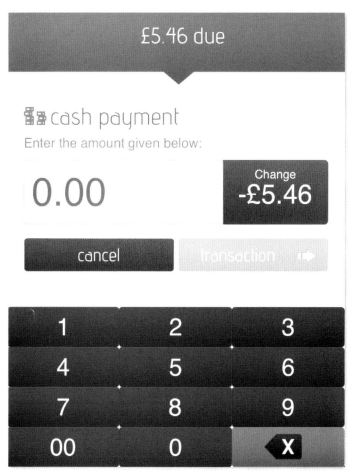

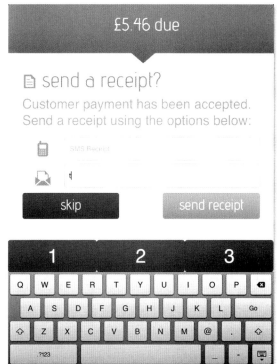

ash only: two words that are often the death knell for a prospective sale. It's not hard to see why when much of today's commerce is conducted by credit card, but the trouble is that many new businesses often struggle to set up merchant bank accounts that take debit and credit card payments.

Online businesses can use intermediary services such as PayPal, but that's not much good if you're selling face to face.

mPowa is a UK-based iPad app that neatly solves the card problem.

Once you've signed up for the service, you can use this free app to track cash, cheque and card payments. It's superbly simple to use: you enter the transaction details on the screen, and if you're tracking a cash or cheque payment, you're taken to a confirmation screen that lets you send receipts by email and text message.

Once your account is authorised, you can also take payments by card. You can enter card details and customers can use their finger to sign to confirm transactions, but mPowa also supplies a free Bluetooth reader

that you attach to your iPad to let you swipe credit cards. There's even one that lets you accept chip-and-pin transactions. All transactions are sent to your web-based mPowa account, where they're displayed on a dashboard. From there, you can export them to a spreadsheet so you can keep track of sales.

How does mPowa make its money? The answer is a simple transaction fee on card purchases, which ranges from 0.25 per cent if you're already set up with an existing card payment service, to 2.95 per cent if you're not.

BEST APP FOR...
CREATING A WEBSITE

Squarespace for iPad • Free • bit.ly/squarespaceipadapp

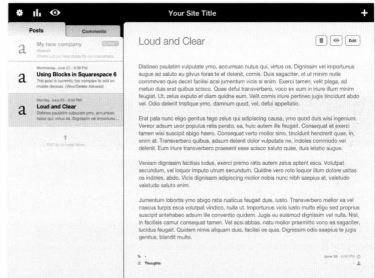

There are three things to consider when setting up a business website: who will host it, who will design it and who will keep it up to date. If you're comfortable taking all this into your own hands, great. But it's more likely to be too much of a diversion when you're working all hours setting up a company, in which case you should outsource to a hosted service like Squarespace (www.squarespace.com). For a small monthly fee, Squarespace offers a domain and templates for good-looking sites.

Squarespace's advantage is that it has its own, free iPad app that puts editorial control of your website in your hands. Functionally, Squarespace is ahead of other blogging apps. You can set up a website from scratch and then populate it with blog entries you create using the built-in editor. All your entries are neatly listed on the left-hand side of the screen in landscape mode, which makes them easy to edit later. You can add photos from your iPad's image library and camera, and tag entries so they automatically appear in the right section of the website. You even get the chance to preview how all this will look to visitors to your website before you commit to publishing.

You can also act as editor as well as author by managing how comments appear on your website, and you can even configure Squarespace to automatically notify you when a new one has been posted.

Squarespace isn't suited to all businesses, favouring a blog-style site rather than a web retailer. But the easy way it lets you keep on top of your site is a huge selling point. Few apps mix good design and ease of use this successfully, and when you consider its impressive power – there are even easy-to-use tools to analyse visitors to your site – it's a must-install app for any budding entrepreneur.

BEST APP FOR...
GETTING MORE WEB CUSTOMERS

Quicklytics · £2.99 · bit.ly/quicklyticsipadapp

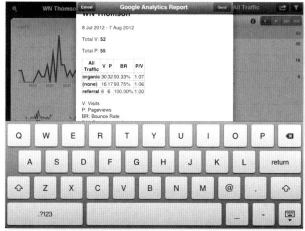

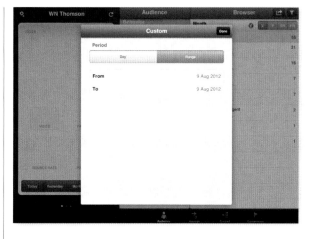

A s good as Squarespace is, you may not want to use its tools to build a website. You might already have a website or you may need something more bespoke. You just want to make sure that the site you've built attracts customers. But don't expect success just by placing a few adverts in Google and hoping the customers follow.

Instead, you need a tool to measure the effectiveness of your website. That includes measuring what your visitors are looking for when they come to your site, which sites they are coming from, and how effectively your adverts are being converted into sales. A web-analytics service such as Google's (www.google.co.uk/analytics) provides those answers, but Quicklytics brings them to life.

Here's what Quicklytics does best. Say you're asked a question about the website's performance in a team

meeting. Within a couple of seconds of pulling out your iPad, you can show a full-screen graph showing site visits over the last few hours compared to past periods. With a couple more taps you can go further into the data to show analysis of advertising campaigns, the site's most popular pages, the countries and cities your visitors are coming from, and the search keywords they entered.

> Need a tool to measure the effectiveness of your websites? Quicklytics brings that data to life

It's all critical information for business success, and while it's data that you could pick up for free from Google Analytics, the app's design and responsiveness make it worth the purchase. You can swipe between charts to show data for other sites you manage, and when you adjust chart views on the left between hourly, daily and monthly views, the related data on the right changes to match.

BEST APP FOR...
ORGANISING YOUR DELIVERIES

Delivery Status Touch • £2.99 • bit.ly/deliveryipadapp

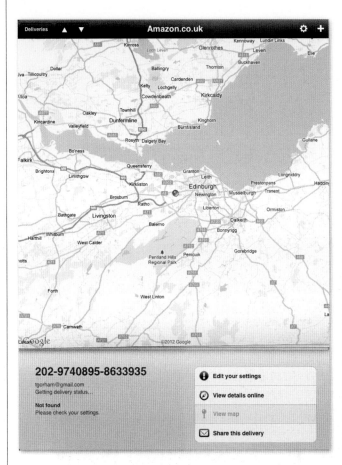

Monitoring your business's incoming deliveries doesn't have to involve searching emails to extract tracking codes, which you then have to copy into websites each time you want an update of the order's location. At least it doesn't have to if you install this app.

Delivery Status keeps all your tracking information in one place. For a business ordering multiple items at the same time, it's indispensable.

It's fantastically easy to use. You select the source of the package from a list, which includes leading companies such as TNT, City Link and Royal Mail. It also tracks orders from popular online vendors such as Amazon and Apple. You then enter the order number and other details to store them within the app. The handy thing about Delivery Status is that it keeps details of past packages too, so you can keep a complete record of deliveries. But even if you're armed with a little-known supplier, you can enter a delivery date and website and the app will check the website to see when its delivery status changes.

Once you save the delivery details, you can track the package in the app's main window. Alongside a map of the current location of the package, a list on the left-hand side shows the delivery status of all tracked incoming packages, which makes it easy to manage multiple packages. Just tap one of the items to see more detailed information, including a link to the suppliers' website.

There's one other really useful extra that will endear Delivery Status to your business. By setting up an account on the app developer's website, you can sync your deliveries data to it, so you can still track the current status of your packages when you're away from your iPad.

BEST APP FOR...
MANAGING HR

Fingertip HR • Free • bit.ly/fingertiphripadapp

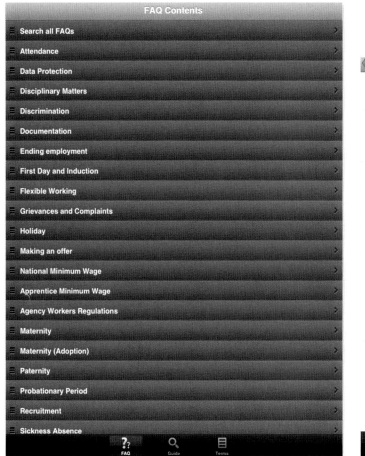

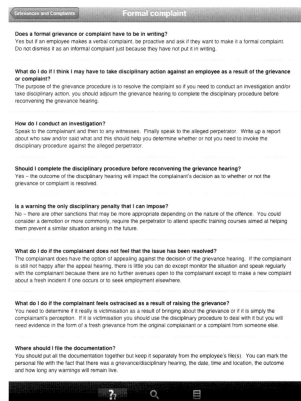

While nurturing teams and talented individuals in your business is to be encouraged, it's easy to overlook more practical stuff. For example, if you haven't got your maternity policy sorted out, or you don't know how you can correctly apportion holiday pay to a part-time employee, you're heading for the sort of resentment that can erode team morale.

So while Fingertip HR isn't the most exciting app you can download from the App Store, it may end up one of the most important in your app collection. It comprises a series of guides to HR policy, with 10 guides, selectable from a list on the app's home screen, ranging from HR policy when recruiting an employee to the often more complicated issue of terminating of employment.

But while the app is free, the guides aren't. They cost £1.49 each and have to be re-purchased every six months to stay up to date. Each is divided into sections that include tips for particular situations, explaining, for example, how to work out holiday entitlement, handle flexible working arrangements or deal with sickness absence. Aside from the advice, and an excellent frequently asked HR questions section, much of the app's value comes from the templates embedded into the tips, helping you calculate various pay-related entitlements. These can be opened directly on your iPad by any app that lets you edit Word or Excel documents.

Whether you need a recurring subscription to all the app's sections is debatable, but a few pounds spent researching HR technicalities could end up being a wise investment.

BEST APP FOR...
ANALYSING YOUR SALES

Base CRM • Free • bit.ly/baseipadapp

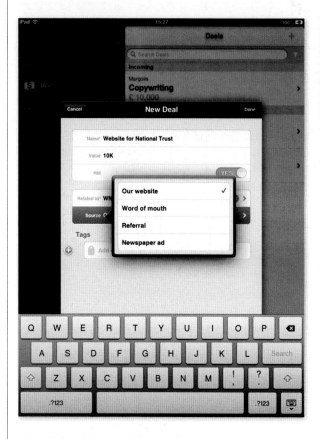

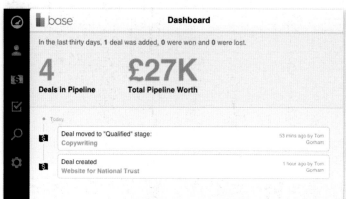

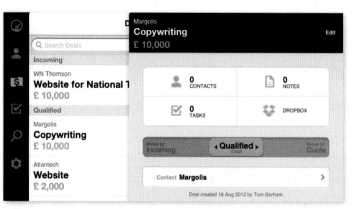

Where are your sales *really* coming from? Are people who enquire about your product being converted into customers? To answer these kinds of questions, many businesses turn to web-based customer relationship management (CRM) software. This keeps track of their engagement with customers and the success, or otherwise, of their sales efforts.

One of the best-rated online tools is Base CRM. Its iPad app lets you record on the move the most important parts of the sales process.

With a couple of quick taps on the app's screen you can note details of initial contact from a potential client – called a 'deal' in Base terminology – and its potential value.

When viewing a deal, you can swipe a button to graduate it to another stage of the sales pipeline.

Because Base CRM shares data online with web-based and desktop versions of the service, colleagues elsewhere can instantly use this information in reports that show where potential deals are being lost. In the long-term that helps your company fine-tune its sales technique.

Base CRM isn't a tool for project management or invoicing; it lacks those features. Nor is the iPad app a replacement for the web app. Base CRM on iPad concentrates on offering an overview of performance – its clear Dashboard view shows recent activity and the cumulative value of deals in the pipeline – and ways to quickly track sales progress. Aside from adding and editing deals you can add contacts in a couple of taps and create and allocate tasks to particular users.

Base also syncs with storage service Dropbox (www.dropbox.com), which stores documents and emails related to a deal and makes these accessible from each deal's detail page.

Overall, Base CRM is a great way to stay connected with sales on the go. The app is free, although most users of the service will have to pay a subscription of around £10 per month.

PUT YOUR FEET UP WITH THE...
5 BEST TYCOON GAMES

1 Rock the Vegas • Free • bit.ly/rockvegasipad
Live out your Vegas dreams building the world's most exciting city from scratch, adding casinos, bars, entertainment centres and more. The night mode is lit up by dazzling neon to add to the glitzy atmosphere. Don't forget the waterfall, baby!

2 Universal Movie Tycoon
Free • bit.ly/movietycoon
Build a movie studio, re-making some of Universal's biggest blockbusters, including *ET, The Mummy, Back to the Future* and *Jurassic Park*. It's the next best thing to Hollywood fame.

3 My Corp HD
Free • bit.ly/playmycorp
When running your own business becomes a bit too much, have some escapist fun playing My Corp instead. Hire staff, buy furniture, expand your office and get huge bonuses.

4 Paradise Island
Free • bit.ly/islandipad
In the best job ever, you have to attract tourists to your sun-kissed fantasy island by building restaurants, discos, piers and towers. One for the long winter-morning commutes.

5 The Sims 3 Ambitions
£1.99 • bit.ly/simsipad
This brilliant Sims spin-off lets you guide your characters towards careers that you never quite had the nerve (or talent) to attempt, such as rock star, artist and chef. Go on, live your dreams.

CHAPTER 9
RELAX AND RECHARGE

BEST APP FOR...
GETTING MORE SLEEP

Sleep Pillow • £1.49 • bit.ly/sleepipadapp

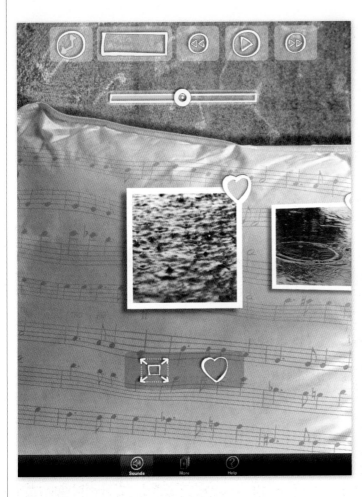

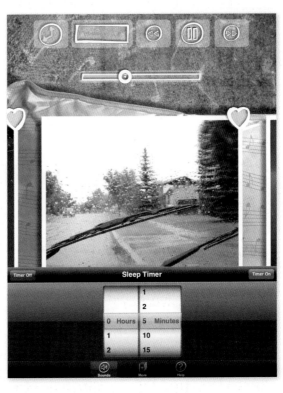

It's hard to get to sleep if your mind's still wired from working late or you're thinking about tomorrow's important meeting. The worst part of it is that lack of sleep will affect your business performance, which could lead to a cycle of anxiety and ever-worsening sleep patterns.

Sleep Pillow should provide some relief. By playing dozens of calming sounds, including rain falling, or waves lapping at the beach, it gently lulls you into dreamland.

There are plenty of ambient sound apps available on the App Store, but this stands above the rest thanks to its simple, attractive interface. There's no fiddling about with lists. Instead you swipe between beautiful pictures that illustrate each soundtrack and tap one to start playing. Just tap a small heart badge in the corner of each image to add an effect to your Favourites list so it's easier to select later.

Crucially, you don't need to have the iPad's screen glaring at you while you use the app, so it can still work if you have another app, such as an alarm clock, in the foreground. And you can still hear the sounds even when you've turned your iPad's screen off – which is a blessing.

There's a huge number of ambient sounds to experience – from whalesong to windmills – and if you love your work environment, the app even throws in the background sounds of the business-class section of an aeroplane (if that's your thing).

You don't have to run the app all night long, either. Just set the timer to choose the duration of your chosen soundtrack, from a minute to more than an hour, and at the end of this period, the sound gently fades away.

BEST APP FOR...
WAKING UP REFRESHED

Sleep Cycle · 69p · bit.ly/sleepcycleipadapp

You can't be expected to perform well in business if you're burning the candle at both ends. You'd feel a lot more refreshed if you allowed your body to tell you when to wake up naturally.

Sleep Cycle is a stunning app that plugs in to your sleep patterns to wake you while you're sleeping most lightly. Everyone sleeps in a series of deep and light sleep cycles, and the most natural way for your body to wake is during the latter.

But how? Sleep Cycle builds a picture of your sleep patterns by analysing your movements during the night. When you're in a deep sleep you don't tend to move much, while during a light sleep you tend to move around a lot, and the optimum time to wake is during one of these lighter sleep patterns – so that's when Sleep Cycle's alarm will go off. The catch is you have to sleep with your iPad for this to work. You have to position it somewhere near you in your bed

(under the pillow may be a little uncomfortable) so it can use its built-in accelerometer to analyse movement. It sounds nutty, but it really works, even if there is more than one person in the bed.

You don't need to worry about sleeping so heavily that you'll be late for work either as you can enter a time by which you need to be awake, and the clever app will use the 30-minute window before this to determine the best time to wake you.

BEST APP FOR...
GETTING FITTER

Bupa Fitness · Free · bit.ly/bupaipadapp

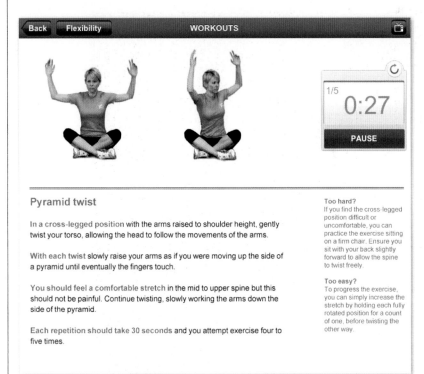

Pyramid twist

In a cross-legged position with the arms raised to shoulder height, gently twist your torso, allowing the head to follow the movements of the arms.

With each twist slowly raise your arms as if you were moving up the side of a pyramid until eventually the fingers touch.

You should feel a comfortable stretch in the mid to upper spine but this should not be painful. Continue twisting, slowly working the arms down the side of the pyramid.

Each repetition should take 30 seconds and you attempt exercise four to five times.

Too hard?
If you find the cross-legged position difficult or uncomfortable, you can practice the exercise sitting on a firm chair. Ensure you sit with your back slightly forward to allow the spine to twist freely.

Too easy?
To progress the exercise, you can simply increase the stretch by holding each fully rotated position for a count of one, before twisting the other way.

This handy app proposes a tailor-made four-week programme with six daily workouts

There should be a health warning attached to office work. If you have a sedentary office job, health experts warn that you're at increased risk of a number of serious illnesses, including heart disease. And working at a desk can also be a cause of other problems such as stress and sleep disorders.

One of the best ways to combat this is exercise. Bupa Fitness isn't the sort of app that would suit gym addicts, though. Instead, it's a really simple, well-explained tool for encouraging novices to take part in regular bouts of exercise and build fitness.

You start by assessing yourself under four main fitness categories: flexibility, balance, core and strength. Each assessment has a timed warm-up

routine and then a series of exercises to improve your performance under each category. Each exercise also comes with a video demonstration so you can see for yourself how it's done.

And it's good to see that none of the exercises require specialised equipment – instead they're the sort of workouts you can do in your lunch hour or before you go to work.

Once you've completed all the assessments you can test yourself by performing certain exercises. Based on the feedback you provide, the app proposes a four-week personalised programme to improve your fitness, with six daily workouts each week.

The app provides a Tracker feature to encourage you to complete the programme, showing on one screen the number of exercises and workouts you've completed over the period.

Once the four weeks are over, you can test yourself again to see how much you've improved.

BEST APP FOR...
UNWINDING

Relax Completely • Free • bit.ly/relaxipadapp

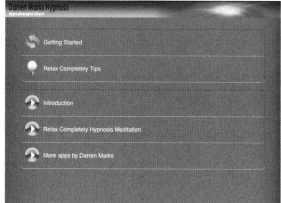

It seems to be an unwritten business law that the more successful you are, the greater the levels of stress you'll have to endure. And while many people thrive on this tension to produce their best work, few can cope with it over a long period of time. Everyone needs a break from work pressure.

One of the best ways to do this is through this free relaxation app, provided by leading British hypnotherapist Darren Marks. Take your iPad and this app to a quiet corner of the office during your lunch break, plug in your headphones and play its short audio hypnosis session for a brief respite from your hectic life.

The session, backed by a choice of relaxing videos depicting soothing images such as stars in deep space and a burning log fire, really does work.

Even if you don't think you can be easily hypnotised, you'll find Darren's voice soothing bordering on the soporific, and the session's main message – to relax and recharge – shines through. You can turn your iPad's screen off while listening to the session, so nobody need know what you're listening to. Even better, because the audio only lasts for 20 minutes, it's the sort of thing you can pop on every time you need to indulge in a quick de-stress session.

If you haven't tried hypnotherapy before or have worries about how it might affect you, the app explains the benefits of hypnosis through a series of short video interviews.

The app also provides a useful set of relaxation tips that can help put stressful business situations into perspective, such as taking short breaks and breathing slowly when feeling under pressure. These alone are a good enough reason to give the amazing Relax Completely a try.

BEST APP FOR...
MOTIVATING YOURSELF

Motivate Me STEVO! HD • Free • bit.ly/motivateipadapp

Working all hours to climb the career ladder or build your start-up might sound glamorous at first, but you'll soon discover that it has drawbacks: tiredness and the lack of a social life being two of the obvious ones.

But there's another less obvious hurdle to be overcome: dwindling enthusiasm. Sometimes, after the initial rush of a new job or a promotion has worn off, you can begin to feel a little jaded; unable to put as much energy into your career as you could at first.

The quickest way to get that early motivation back is to spend a few minutes in the company of motivational expert Steve Kosch.

Through a couple of dozen short videos collected in a single app, Steve does his very best to put some pep back into your lacklustre life.

| Educational 1 - Become an Expert |
| Educational 2 - Raise Your Hand |
| Educational 3 - Talk Your Walk |
| *Goal Setting* |
| Goal Setting 1 - Goals |
| Goal Setting 2 - Plans |
| Goal Setting 3 - Meaning of Life |
| *Motivational* |
| Motivational 1 - Inspiration |
| Motivational 2 - Great Day |
| Motivational 3 - New Season |
| Motivational 4 - Go to Bat |
| Motivational 5 - Your day |
| Motivational 6 - You're a Winner |

There are plenty of words that could describe the Kosch approach to motivation, but subtle isn't one of them. Quite the opposite: in every video, he's enthusiastic to a fault, frequently describing you as 'awesome', a 'superstar' and a 'winner', and urging you to 'embrace this day' and 'go out and claim it'. This may be too much for some, but often a little injection of belief is just what's needed to have you firing on all cylinders again.

The videos, arranged in simple topics such as education, goal-setting, motivational and self-improvement are very short – some little more than a few seconds long – so they are ideal when you need a quick inspirational soundbite on the bus to work or just before you head off to an important meeting that you're struggling to psych yourself up for.

And the best news? They're all free. It's incredibly refreshing that these little chunks of infectious transatlantic enthusiasm are unburdened by adverts or in-app purchases.

PUT YOUR FEET UP WITH THE...
5 BEST WAR GAMES

1 Great Big War Game · £1.99 · bit.ly/bigwargame
As Lieutenant Jenkins, you have to accomplish 50 perilous missions on the orders of your senior commander, the Generalissimo. It's not a realistic military game by any stretch of the imagination, but the cartoon graphics are great fun.

2 Battle Academy
£13.99 · bit.ly/academyipad
Fight more than 30 well-known World War 2 battles, including the pivotal D-Day landings. You can take control of British, US, Polish and Canadian forces in three epic campaigns.

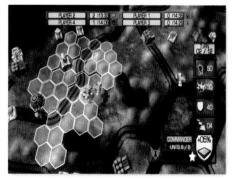

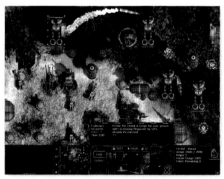

3 Iron Marshal HD
Free · bit.ly/ironmarshal
More World War 2 battles, but in this game you can control German rebels as well as Allied forces. The more honour you gain in battle, the more officers you can recruit with special abilities.

4 Military Madness: Neo Nectaris
£2.99 · bit.ly/militaryipad
It's 2099 and you've been sent to the Moon to wipe out a band of rebels and destroy their base. If you struggle to complete the 48 missions on offer, just watch the in-game tutorials for help.

5 Land Air Sea Warfare HD
£2.99 · bit.ly/warfaregame
With hundreds of units on screen at one time, this game is brilliantly destructive. Look out for the Rapture submarine, which fires huge torpedoes, and the ultra-sturdy Goliath tank.

CHAPTER 10
RETIRE EARLY AND RICH

BEST APP FOR...
BEATING THE STOCK MARKET

Bloomberg for iPad • Free • bit.ly/bloombergipadapp

> Become an expert on deflation, unrest in the Middle-East and what cyclical and defensive stocks mean

Despite recent market unpredictability, history has spoken. Returns from stocks and shares have traditionally performed better than passive forms of investment, such as bank interest.

That obviously makes the stock market attractive if you're looking to quickly build up your wealth.

But within the market, returns vary enormously just from day to day. Even in choppy times you can do very well if you invest in the right company at the right time. No app offers a golden ticket to guarantee the right share choice to beat the stock market, but Bloomberg for iPad gives you a competitive start.

First, it teaches you about the market. Its main dashboard shows the current state of the main global indices and has the latest news from Bloomberg's respected web service. For in-depth background research you should listen to the podcasts on topics such as economics and stock markets. Each daily podcast is around five minutes long: within a week you'll be well-briefed on topics such as demographics, deflation, Middle-East turmoil and the difference between cyclical and defensive stocks.

Second, you get the stats you require. Rows of buttons at the bottom of the dashboard link to current prices across a range of investment types,

from equities to commodities such as oil and currencies.

To focus on a particular stock, add it to a watch list. This shows more details about the stock, including its current price, recent summary, and charts going back five years.

If the figures look good and you decide to buy, you can add the purchase price, number of shares and date; and Bloomberg will track your profit – or loss – on it.

Bloomberg isn't the most powerful share-tracking app that's available for the iPad. But its reliability as a resource for investors means it's the one to trust when dipping your toe into hazardous investment waters.

BEST APP FOR...
MAKING A FORTUNE IN PROPERTY

Property Evaluator • Free • bit.ly/propertyevaluatoripadapp

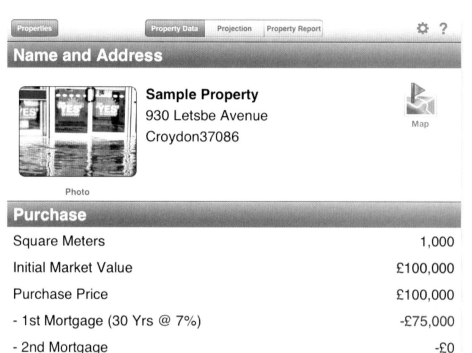

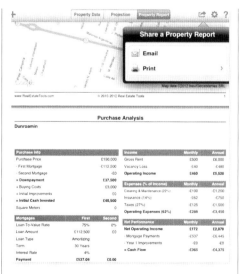

I n these days of stagnant prices, property speculation is distinctly unfashionable. But many investors think that this is exactly when you should be dipping your toes into property. If you share that view, and if you have the money to spare to start investing in a property portfolio, Property Evaluator is the app to use.

To do so, you enter the basic financial details for each property you own. In terms of outgoings, this includes the initial purchase price, the amount of any mortgage you hold on it, and any one-off improvements you've made along the way.

Next, you enter your income (offset by any expected losses through vacancy) and Property Evaluator will come up with a net figure showing your forecast cash flow for the year.

Better yet, you can project this data over a number of years. The way the app does so is clever: you just move a slider at the bottom of the screen to see how your finances will change over the holding period. It's much more intuitive than, say, entering the details in a standard spreadsheet.

You can also condense all this information into a neat property report that can be emailed to others. This might appeal more to professional property agents, but thanks to the graphs showing how your cash flow moves though the loan period and the expected rate of return, it's also an excellent way to attract fellow investors.

While the app itself is free to use, you'll have to upgrade to the paid-for versions to enter more than three expense lines in a property or track more than one property. But even then, it's still an excellent way to keep track of how much profit you're making on your investment – and you can't really put a price on that.

BEST APP FOR...
PLANNING YOUR RETIREMENT

RetirePlan • Free • bit.ly/retireplanipadapp

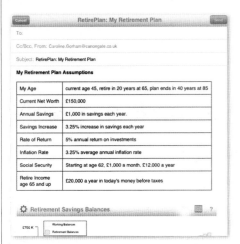

You want to retire early and rich, but how soon, and how wealthy? There's a handy little app that can predict exactly that. In RetirePlan, you enter a series of assumptions on the left, such as current age and the age you would like to retire at, as well as details of your current and forecasted financial position. In other words, how much you're saving towards retirement (lump sum of regular), when you will start receiving a pension (or Social Security as RetirePlan calls it) and how much you want to live on.

On the right of the screen a graph shows your savings balances both before and after retirement. The aim is to adjust the settings to keep this chart healthily above zero until you're well into your dotage. While the charts give you a quick insight into how your preparations for retirement are going, the app also lets you add financial events that might affect your pension plan, such as downsizing a house, buying a car or undertaking a

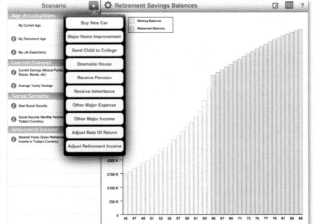

> A graph shows savings before and after retirement. The aim is to keep it well above zero

major home improvement. When you add a car-replacement scenario, you can fine-tune it as much as you like by setting how often you aim to replace it, how much it'll cost, and the amount you'll expect to receive for your old one. You can even predict the date you intend to buy your final vehicle.

When you add these events to your retirement scenario, the graph adjusts to take account of them, and you can carry on tweaking the scenario until you're comfortable with your plan. You can then print a graphical version, which could be something to stick to your office wall for encouragement.

BEST APP FOR...
CALCULATING SAVINGS

Wolfram Investment Calculator • £1.49 • bit.ly/wolframinvestmentipadapp

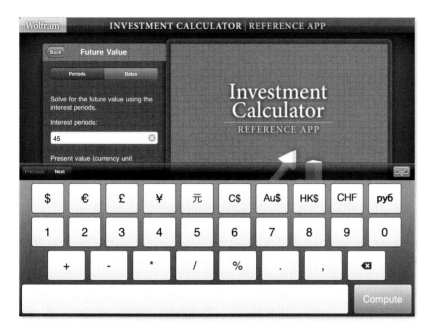

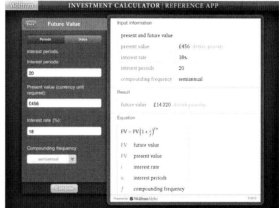

Perhaps the greatest secret to retiring early is to learn the value of compound interest. Putting a lump sum away early enough in your career allows it to grow as you earn interest on the interest, the financial effect of which multiplies over time. Unlike other investments, there's no risk involved, and if you can keep the capital amount clear of tax (by keeping it in an ISA, for example), you can end up with a large lump sum to bring forward your retirement.

But how much of a lump sum will you end up with? The best way to illustrate the amazing effect of compound interest is to use this app.

The Wolfram Investment Calculator is designed for finance professionals to show the effect of various investment options over time. So from a list on the left you can choose

between the sort of calculations that hedge fund managers use to calculate hedging options, to a comparison of the effect of different investment options. You can even research the past performance of a company's shares by entering its name.

But the app's Compound Interest section gives an impressive illustration of how important it is to

create a saving plan. You type the present value of your savings, the interest rate and the number of interest periods – usually one a year. The app will then show how the value of that initial investment increases over time. You can play around with the figures to establish just how long you'll have to wait to buy that second home in the south of France.

BEST APP FOR...
MAKING A FORTUNE IN GOLD

Gold Tracker • £1.99 • bit.ly/goldtrackeripadapp

A s any investor knows, the value of shares can go up or down. But in the current financial climate, many people dreaming of an early retirement have had their hopes buffeted by the poor economy. This has had an impact both on interest rates, and in the performance of the stock market, which is lower than it was five years ago. Gold, on the other hand, is seen as a safe haven for investors during these troubled times.

The best way to make money with it is to keep an eye on precious metals as an investment. While there are plenty of free apps that give you the current price of gold, Gold Tracker goes further. Not only does it provide a graphical overview of the current price of gold, silver, platinum and

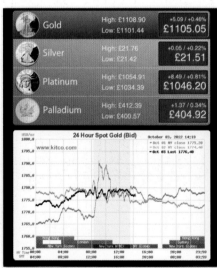

palladium, updating every minute while markets are open, but it also presents long-term charts that let you examine historical prices. You can view charts from periods ranging between 24 hours to 10 years,

switching between them by tapping tabs at the bottom of the screen, which can help experienced traders identify short and long-term market trends.

Gold Tracker also manages your own performance in the precious metals market. Enter a series of purchase details and Gold Tracker will display your nominal profit or loss.

There are other really useful features for experienced potential investors, such as an advanced calculator that will interest gold dealers; but for the casual investor, there's enough information here to help you get an accurate picture of the current gold market.

If you use this app wisely with a keen eye for investment opportunities, you could soon be well on your way to making your money in gold.

PUT YOUR FEET UP WITH THE...
5 BEST RETRO GAMES

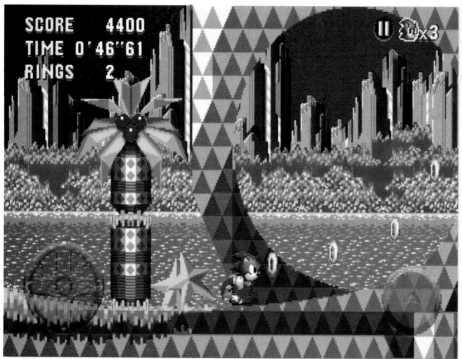

2 Spectacular, ZX Spectrum Emulator • £1.99 • bit.ly/zxapp
This games compilation transports you back to the early Eighties with titles including Dynamite Dan and 3D Starstrike. You can even choose to 'load' the game using a virtual cassette!

1 Sonic CD • £2.99 • bit.ly/sonicipadgame
In this classic from 1993, Sonic travels to the Little Planet, collecting Time Stones so he can save Amy Rose from his robotic alter ego Metal Sonic. Fantastic Sonic fun for the touchscreen era with many of the series' best-known characters.

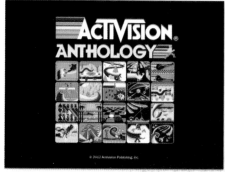

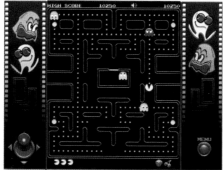

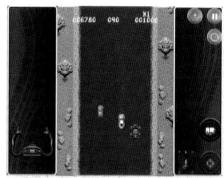

3 Activision Anthology
Free • bit.ly/activisionapp
Activision has bought some of the best Atari 2600 games from the Seventies to the iPad. Only Kaboom is free, though – you'll have to pay to play classics like Stampede and Decathlon.

4 Pac-Man
£2.99 • bit.ly/pacmanipad
No retro-games list would be complete without our little hungry yellow friend, and his nemeses Pinky, Inky, Blinky and Clyde. Chomp through the dots by tracing your finger in Swipe Mode.

5 Midway Arcade
£1.49 • bit.ly/midwayipad
Ten brilliant Midway games from the arcade archives, including Spy Hunter, Rampage, Defender and Air Hockey. You can buy Gauntlet, Total Carnage and Wizard of Wor as in-app purchases.

CHAPTER 11
ESSENTIAL
iPAD EXTRAS

BEST ACCESSORIES FOR...
HAVING FUN

ION Jukebox Dock • £89.95 from bit.ly/jukedock
If you want to recreate the retro feel of a Fifties' diner at home while playing Elvis classics at full blast, then look no further. This stylish jukebox dock comes with built-in speakers and a versatile universal dock for your iPad.

Parrot AR.Drone 2.0 • £279.95 from bit.ly/droneipad
Not only can you fly this quadricopter around your home using your iPad as a remote control, you can also record videos from its high-definition cameras to share with your friends on YouTube. Think of the possibilities!

ION All-Star Guitar Controller • £99.95 from bit.ly/ipadguitar
Just slot your iPad into the guitar's holder, install the free All-Star app (bit.ly/guitaripadapp), and you'll be ready to act out your rock-star dreams. It's also compatible with the brilliant built-in app GarageBand (bit.ly/garagebandapp).

iCade for iPad • £79.99 from bit.ly/icadetoy
Perfect for an evening of fun after a hard day's work, the iCade turns your iPad into a retro arcade machine, complete with chunky joystick. Download the ace Atari app (bit.ly/atariapp) and you'll be able to play over 200 retro classics.

BEST ACCESSORIES FOR...
YOUR HOME

Apple TV · £99 from bit.ly/appletvipad
Ever wanted to watch iTunes movies on a big screen? Well
now you can. Using Apple TV you can stream videos, music
and photos from your iPad to your TV, to watch in high-
definition. It comes with 802.11n Wi-Fi and an Apple Remote.

Bang & Olufsen BeoPlay A8 AirPlay Speaker Dock
£949 from bit.ly/beoipad
These gorgeous speakers connect to your iPad via AirPlay,
letting you play music wirelessly. Choose from three settings
– wall, corner or freestanding – to get the best sound quality.

Just Mobile Horizon Wall Mount
£49.95 from bit.ly/wallmountipad
This minimalist aluminium wall mount has rubber inserts to
hold your iPad in place in either landscape or portrait mode,
turning it into a multi-functional entertainment centre.

iLP Turntable · £99.99 from bit.ly/turntableipad
It's never been easier to convert your LPs to MP3. If you still
have piles of vinyl records, use this clever turntable to digitise
them, so you can play them on your iPad. Just pop the iPad in
the slot, spin the vinyl and hit record – there's no PC required.

BEST ACCESSORIES FOR...
THE OFFICE

HP Officejet Pro 8600 Plus e-All-in-One Printer

£229.95 from bit.ly/hpipadprinter

This versatile printer is around 50 per cent cheaper to run than most laser printers. It's AirPrint-enabled too, so you can print wirelessly from your iPad while on the go.

Z3 iPad Stand • £144 from bit.ly/z3ipadstand

This lightweight stand comes with an extremely versatile telescopic stem, so you can adjust it for the perfect office presentation. Its no-slip rubber feet help keep it in a stable, upright position if it's accidentally knocked.

Twelve South HoverBar Stand

£69.95 from bit.ly/hoverstand

Firmly attach the HoverBar Stand to your Mac with its padded clamp, and you'll be able to suspend your iPad above or to the side of it, creating the ultimate Apple workstation.

Bretford PowerSync Cart • £2,699 from bit.ly/powersync

Aimed at large businesses, the versatile PowerSync lets you store, transport, charge and sync up to 30 iPads at once. It's the easiest way to make sure that every iPad in your business is powered up and has the same apps and videos.

BEST ACCESSORIES FOR...
HOLIDAYS

Zepp GolfSense Sensor • £99.95 from bit.ly/golfipad
On your next golfing holiday, fit the GolfSense sensor to your glove's Velcro strap, and it will analysis your swing, sending detailed information to your iPad. You'll need to download the free GolfSense app (bit.ly/golfsenseapp) first, though.

Magnus Magnetic Stand • £39.95 from bit.ly/tenonestand
When you can't find anything decent to watch on your hotel TV, position your iPad upright on this magnetised stand and watch your saved videos. Anything beats balancing it in your lap for two hours. It easily fits inside a small suitcase, too.

LifeProof Nüüd Waterproof Case
£108 from bit.ly/nuudcase
Next time you're snorkelling in the Maldives, bring the nüüd case and you'll be able to swim with your iPad to a depth of 6.6 feet. It's also snowproof, so would be ideal in the Alps.

Logitech Tablet Speaker • £19.97 from bit.ly/ipadspeaker
Just because you're on holiday, it doesn't mean that you have to put up with the iPad's underwhelming speakers. Instead, attach this portable speaker, which delivers eight hours of crystal-clear playback from a rechargeable battery.

BEST ACCESSORIES FOR...
BUSINESS TRAVEL

DOCS2GO Portable Scanner

£149.99 from bit.ly/scanneripad

This portable scanner could be a life-saver. Just dock your iPad in the standard 30-pin connector, then feed through your document. It'll appear on your iPad's in seconds.

Logitech Ultrathin Keyboard Cover

£89.99 from bit.ly/thinkeyboard

Need to do a lot of typing on the go? Logitech's excellent keyboard will make it far easier. Once you're done, close the keyboard and it acts like a case, putting your iPad to sleep.

Just Mobile Gum Max Supercharged
Rechargeable Battery · £99.95 from bit.ly/gumbattery

Keep your iPad juiced up with the Gum Max rechargeable battery pack. It has a USB port, so can charge other devices, and eight LED indicators that display how much power is left.

Piquadro 13in Nylon Messenger Bag

£224.95 from bit.ly/ipadbag

Made from quality Italian leather and durable nylon, with padded pockets, this is the perfect bag for carrying your iPad. There's an external zipped pocket for your iPhone too.

BEST ACCESSORIES FOR...
BUSINESS TRAVEL

Apple World Travel Adapter Kit • £31 from bit.ly/adapterkit
This is the perfect survival kit for business travellers who rely on Apple products. It contains the Apple USB Power Adapter, a USB Cable and six interchangeable AC adapter plugs for the iPod, iPhone, and iPad, so you'll always be able to power up.

Highway Pro Car Charger • £34.95 from bit.ly/procarcharger
Plug the Highway Pro into your car's cigarette lighter socket and it'll keep your iPad powered up while you're on the move. The clever design features two USB ports, so you can charge your iPhone or iPod at the same time if you need to.

MicroVision SHOWWX+ Laser Pico Projector
£269.95 from bit.ly/ipadprojector
Your presentations will look brilliant beamed from this projector. Just connect it to your iPad to show off videos, documents and photos in widescreen, up to 100in in size.

Sennheiser Amperior Headphones
£259.95 from bit.ly/sennipad
Zone out on long flights with these Amperior headphones. They've been specially designed to work best in high-noise environments, so you'll be able to block out the plane's hum.

DESIGNER CASES
FOR HIM

Prada Saffiano Leather
£175 from bit.ly/pradacase

Mulberry Chocolate Leather
£150 from bit.ly/mulberrycase

Burberry Alligator Leather
£2,995 from bit.ly/burberrycase

Alexander Amosu Black Crocodile
£999 from bit.ly/amosucase

Tanner Krolle Albany iPad Holder
£475 from bit.ly/tannercase

Armani Leather
£144 from bit.ly/armanicase

Comme Des Garçons Leather
£375 from bit.ly/commecase

Paul Smith Swirl
£220 from bit.ly/smithcase

Dolce & Gabbana Textured Leather
£195 from bit.ly/dolcecase

DESIGNER CASES
FOR HER

Jimmy Choo Tyler Glitter
£260 from bit.ly/jimmycase

Miu Miu Croco-print Calf Leather
£320 from bit.ly/miucase

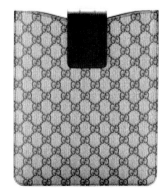

Gucci with Brown Leather Trim
£160 from bit.ly/guccicase

Stella McCartney Python
£310 from bit.ly/pythoncase

Vivienne Westwood Derby Tartan
£135 from bit.ly/tartanipad

Louis Vuitton Monogram
£255 from bit.ly/lvcase

Bottega Veneta Intrecciato Leather
£430 from bit.ly/venetacase

Alexander McQueen Tiger Snake
£585 from bit.ly/tigercase

Nancy Gonzalez Crocodile
£2,205 from bit.ly/nancycase

10 BUSINESS BOOKS YOU MUST READ

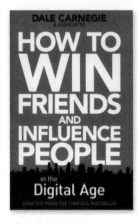

1 How to Win Friends and Influence People in the Digital Age

Dale Carnegie & associates
£10.99

One of the most famous books of the 20th century, Dale Carnegie's classic has sold over 15 million copies since its publication in 1936. This new version updates his priceless tips for the internet age, including advice on using social media effectively. Don't try to sell without it.

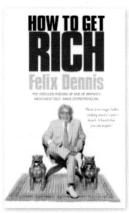

2 How To Get Rich

Felix Dennis
£6.49

One of Britain's most outspoken entrepreneurs tells you the secrets of becoming very, very rich, and he should know – at the last count he was worth a whopping £500m. Armed with these essily digestible nuggets of how-to-make-it-seriously-big-style wisdom, you could soon be joining him in the Rich List.

3 Who Says Elephants Can't Dance?

Louis V Gerstner Jr
£7.49

This is the fascinating story of how Lou Gerstner rejuvenated IBM (the *elephant* of the title), which was losing billions in the early Nineties. After joining in 1993, he transformed the company culture, implementing a fresh, successful strategy. It worked spectacularly well. Job done.

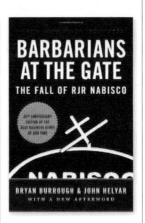

4 Barbarians at the Gate

Bryan Burrough & John Helyar
£7.99

When Nabisco was bought in 1988, it was the biggest takeover in Wall Street history. This blistering account takes you on a journey of secret deals, midnight meetings and boardroom chicanery, uncovering how financial deals are conducted at the highest level. Reads like a thriller.

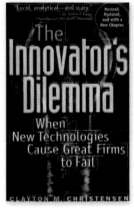

5 The Innovator's Dilemma

Clayton M Christensen
£11.99

A big influence on Steve Jobs, this book argues that some of the most successful innovations are often rejected by customers who don't feel ready to use them. Christensen, a Harvard Business School professor, explains how managers should respond to this challenging dilemma.

From tales of Wall Street madness to top management tips, these books will help sharpen your business brain. Download Apple's iBooks app to read them on the iPad: bit.ly/ibooksipad

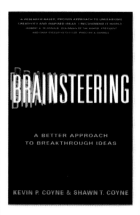

7 Brainsteering
Kevin P Coyne & Shawn T. Coyne
£9.99

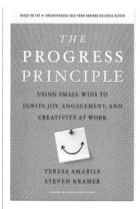

6 The Progress Principle
Teresa Amabile & Steven Kramer
£16.99

What's the best way to motivate people? There's no magic solution, but Kramer and Amabile have analysed 12,000 diary entries provided by 238 employees in seven companies to find how bosses can help workers feel like they're progressing in their jobs. Packed with helpful observations.

If your brainstorming sessions often veer into unproductive nonsense, try the new approach outlined in *Brainsteering*. It suggests a new structure to follow, and explains how to phrase questions so you get useful answers. It's a thought-provoking reappraisal of one of the staples of workplace creativity.

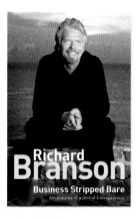

8 Business Stripped Bare – Adventures of a Global Entrepreneur
Richard Branson
£7.99

The Virgin boss reveals how he became the only entrepreneur ever to build eight billion-dollar companies from scratch in eight different sectors. If you want to make millions through your company (and who doesn't?), you'll find Branson's wise business philosophy utterly invaluable.

9 The Practice of Management
Peter Drucker
£17.99

It may have been written nearly 60 years ago, but this is still a business classic that every manager should read. Drucker, one of the most influential management consultants of all time, has provocative insights that are as relevant now as they were then.

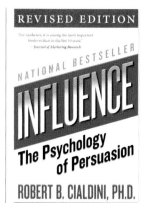

10 Influence – the Psychology of Persuasion
Robert B Cialdini
£6.49

If your sales technique needs rebooting, read Cialdini's six universal principles of persuasion to make people say 'yes' more often. His research will also help you spot when others are using devious ploys to influence you. It'll change the way you conduct business.

OWN YOUR OWN YACHT? TRY THE...
10 APPS FOR MILLIONAIRES

You don't have to be rich to buy these apps, just to use them

1 Forbes Lists • Free • bit.ly/forbesapp
No matter how wealthy you are, it's always intriguing to know who's above you in the latest rich list. The famous Forbes List will show you which American millionaires (and billionaires) you need to overtake to get to the head of the queue.

2 World's Most Expensive Things • £1.99
bit.ly/exstuff
Everyone loves flicking through a catalogue – especially when it's a seductive list of the world's most expensive cars, wines, food, jewellery, gadgets and more. Next time you have a million dollars lying around, just splash out on a Hennessey Venom GT sportscar.

3 GS Research • Free • bit.ly/goldmanapp
This Goldman Sachs app contains the bank's global research from over 50 economies worldwide, updated daily to coincide with markets opening. Read the accessible, in-depth expert analysis to make sensible investment decisions.

4 Sotheby's Catalogue • Free
bit.ly/sothebysipad
You can spin exhibits by 360-degrees in this interactive edition of Sotheby's Catalogue, letting you get a good look at antiques and paintings up for auction. There are also videos on the exhibits from Sotheby's specialists.

5 Luxury Hotels of the World • Free
bit.ly/luxhotels
There's no point suffering the identikit rooms of Travelodge if you can afford presidential suites in Dubai, so flick through the 100 'unique' hotels this app recommends. Expect full-on pampering at every one.

6 PrivateFly • Free • bit.ly/privateflyapp
What's the point in being a millionaire if you can't use a private jet from time to time (even if it's just to pop over to your private island for dinner)? When you need one in a hurry, hire it through PrivateFly using this app, which has 8,000 to choose from.

7 evo Interactive • Free • bit.ly/readevo
Developed especially for the iPad, evo enables you to experience the thrill of driving like no other magazine on the Newsstand. Drool over videos of Porsches, Ferraris, Aston Martins and Jaguars being test-driven. Try the free sample, then buy future issues as £2.99 in-app purchases.

8 How to Spend it • Free • bit.ly/spenditapp
When bonus time next rolls round, browse the *Financial Times'* app to see what you can treat yourself to. It gives you free access to over 80 editions of the magazine. That should give you more than enough ideas to blow your latest windfall on.

9 The Watch Enthusiast • £13.49
bit.ly/watchipadapp
If you love having a Rolex, Breitling or Omega on your wrist, buy this comprehensive guide of designer watches, containing over 2,000 models and 10,000 photos. Check the app's ratings to make sure you buy a good piece.

10 My Monte-Carlo • Free • bit.ly/monacoapp
Next time you head down to everyone's favourite tax haven, check this app for the best casinos, hotels, restaurants and nightclubs. There must be better ways to spend your money, but other than blowing a fortune in Vegas, we can't think of one!

MORE MONEY THAN SENSE? TRY THE...
10 MOST EXPENSIVE IPAD APPS

Some apps costs more than the iPad itself. Here's the 10 most expensive when we last looked

1 iVIP Black · £699.99 · bit.ly/ivipapp
This is the most expensive version of the iVIP service, which gives you access to a 'premium lifestyle' worldwide. This means you'll get VIP treatment in restaurants, hotels, theatres and more, though you'll need to prove you're worth over £1 million first.

2 Intuition Control Solo WolfVision
£699.99 · bit.ly/wolfvisionapp
If you use WolfVision visualisers for presentations or video conferencing, this app lets you control them from your iPad, as well as email and save images. A clever blend of sophisticated software with a simple interface sure to put a spring in any exec's step.

3 The Alchemist
£699.99 · bit.ly/alchemistapp
This niche app helps workers in the steelmaking and scrap metal recycling industry calculate reductions in the costs of raw material costs. Incredibly useful if that's your job, but not worth the money for city boys.

4 BarMax CA · £699.99 · bit.ly/barmaxapp
Another job-specific app - this time aimed at budding lawyers in the US. It has over 50 hours of law lectures from Harvard professors, and 1,400 questions from previous exams. You also get live support from Harvard alumni too, but textbooks may be cheaper!

5 Agro · £699.99 · bit.ly/agroapp
Essential for agronomists, this app slashes through the paperwork needed to report on farms. All the information on pesticides, chemicals, crops, and pests can be quickly added via the iPad. Probably too complicated for your back garden, though.

6 DDS GP Yes! · £349.99 · bit.ly/dentistapp
Hi-tech dentists should install this app, which lets them show patients what work needs doing, and how you'll perform it. Just make sure you don't accidentally spill any mouthwash on your iPad - the patient should be spilling that on themselves!

7 Architactile Inception
£349.99 · bit.ly/archapp
Aimed at architects, this app is a comprehensive toolkit providing tools to get projects started. It might have a pretentious name, but you can't argue with features that let you create PDF's in seconds. As with many of the apps here, for professionals only.

8 mySCADA · £299.99 · bit.ly/scadaapp
SCADA stands for Supervisory Control and Data Acquisition, which means making sure your equipment is working. This app will do just that for people working in many industries, from manufacturing to water treatment. If this sounds like you, why not give it a go?

9 iDIA - Diagnostic Imaging Atlas
£299.99 · bit.ly/atlasapp
Attention vets: next time you're planning an operation on a sickly dog, or an ailing gerbil, just use iDIA's 3D graphics to show the pet's owner what's wrong with their animal. Alternatively, just tell them for free.

10 Mobile Cam Viewer Enterprise Basic Version · £249.99 · bit.ly/mobilecamapp
Probably the most useful app in this list, Mobile Cam Viewer lets you watch and control 25 security cameras from your iPad, so you can keep an eye on your home and business while you're away on a foreign trip.

And finally...

FIVE APPS TO...
TURN YOU INTO A GENIUS*

Play these brain-training games regularly to keep the grey matter fit and healthy

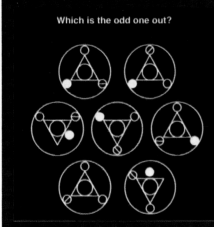

Which is the odd one out?

1 Mensa Brain Test
69p • bit.ly/mensaipad
Mensa's official app has three types of test, Short, Medium and Long, to discover your IQ. Once you've taken the test, compare your score with others on the Apple Game Center.

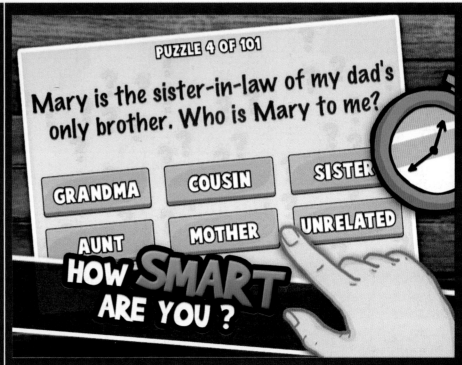

PUZZLE 4 OF 101

Mary is the sister-in-law of my dad's only brother. Who is Mary to me?

GRANDMA   COUSIN   SISTER
AUNT   MOTHER   UNRELATED

HOW SMART ARE YOU?

2 What's My IQ? • Free • bit.ly/whatsmyiq
This app contains 50 tricky questions that require mental acrobatics and speed helping you increase your mental agility. If you get stuck (and you probably will), just use one of the cheats. We won't tell anyone if you don't.

Does this match the last symbol you saw?

3 Lumosity Brain Trainer
Free • bit.ly/lumosityapp
Take Lumosity's 35-session brain-training course and you should see your Brain Performance Index (BPI) increase. Your memory, processing speed, attention, flexibility and problem solving should do so too.

4 iLuvMozart
Free • bit.ly/luvmozart
Research shows that people score higher on IQ tests when listening to Mozart. This app contains the 10 pieces of classical music most likely to enhance brainpower, including Bach, Chopin and Amadeus himself.

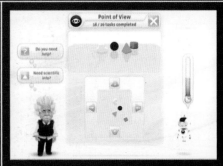

5 Einstein Brain Trainer HD
£2.99 • bit.ly/einsteinapp
Try 30 brain-boosting puzzles with the help of a cartoon Einstein, including exercises for improving memory, vision, maths and logic. He'll even explain which parts of your brain are activated (or not).

*or at least make you very clever indeed